How easy it is to abstract our study how deadly. In this volume we are c with godly wisdom both from spiritι ...ay and mature scholars of today. Teachers of tl ...ures need mentors so that we are refreshed by God's presence and power in our studies. I was consoled, convicted, instructed, and even ushered into God's presence by this book.

THOMAS R. SCHREINER
James Buchanan Harrison Professor of New Testament Interpretation
The Southern Baptist Theological Seminary, Louisville, Kentucky

When I began my theological studies in 1968 I devoured Helmut Thielicke's *A Little Exercise for Young Theologians*. If I were starting today I would devour *The Trials of Theology*. Here is counsel from the proven dead and the wise living. 'Do we need to do theology?' We may as well ask, 'Do we need to know God?' Ten thousand times yes. 'Is studying theology perilous?' Yes. But less perilous than ignorance. 'Will it be costly?' Let the Bible answer: 'It is good for me that I was afflicted, that I might learn your statutes' [Ps. 119:71]. Without the 'trials of theology' we remain on the surface of the statutes of God. May the Spirit of truth make this book a means of true thinking about God, deep affections for God, and beautiful obedience to God, through Jesus Christ who is God.

JOHN PIPER
Pastor for Preaching and Vision,
Bethlehem Baptist Church, Minneapolis, Minnesota

The title *The Trials of theology* may sound curious to some, but for those who have devoted themselves to the study of the Bible and Christian theology there will be instant resonance – because such work, however exalted, is freighted with unique snares and dark chasms. And here the authors have assembled under one cover the sagest voices of the centuries, past to the present, to guide the church in this perilous pursuit. Reading these chapters is a veritable feast of finely wrought essays and homilies packed with memorable quotations and epigrams that will invite repeated visits. I only wish that this treasury of wisdom had been there for me when I began my theological studies. This is the book that so many of us have been waiting for, a book that will be sure to grace the lives of students and pastors and their teachers in the years to come.

R. KENT HUGHES
Senior Pastor Emeritus
College Church, Wheaton, Illinois

THE **TRIALS** OF

BECOMING A 'PROVEN WORKER'
IN A DANGEROUS BUSINESS

EDITED BY
ANDREW J. B. CAMERON AND BRIAN S. ROSNER

CHRISTIAN
FOCUS

Copyright © Andrew J.B. Cameron and Brian S. Rosner 2010

ISBN 978-1-84550-467-0

10 9 8 7 6 5 4 3 2 1

Published in 2010
by
Christian Focus Publications,
Geanies House, Fearn,
Ross-shire, IV20 1TW, Scotland
www.christianfocus.com

Cover Design by Paul Lewis

Printed by Bell & Bain Ltd., Glasgow

Mixed Sources
Product group from well-managed
forests and other controlled sources
www.fsc.org   Cert no. TT-COC-002769
© 1996 Forest Stewardship Council

CONTENTS

About the editors
Andrew Cameron and Brian Rosner both teach at Moore Theological College (www.moore.edu.au) in Sydney, Australia. This book complements *The Consolations of Theology* (Eerdmans, 2008), which Brian edited and to which Andrew contributed.

Lost Among Words

Is the study of theology best avoided? This book is for those who study theology, and for those who having studied it now 'use' it on a 'professional' basis. Are they in danger?

'There is perhaps hardly a theological student,' wrote Helmut Thielicke, 'who has not been earnestly and emphatically warned by some pious soul against the dubious undertaking' called theological study. We can tend to dismiss such warnings as somehow uninformed. 'If the theologian, however, does not take more seriously the objections of the washerwoman and the simple hourly-wage earner' then 'surely something is not right with theology'.[1] These warnings come from somewhere and alert us to something real.

I first seriously studied theology in the early 1990s. I was in my late twenties at the time, and the experience was completely life-changing. Questions I had often asked about Jesus, God and the Bible were answered. The interconnections between biblical language and history, theological reflection, and my relationship with God were forged, reformed, strengthened and renewed. My world was revolutionised.

---

1. Helmut Thielicke, *A Little Exercise for Young Theologians*, tr. Charles L. Taylor (Grand Rapids: Eerdmans, 1962), pp. 3, 4.

But there were some odd moments. Old doubts would disappear, but new worries replaced them, and weeks would pass when I felt quite at sea. I vividly remember one very strange experience, when all the theological words became detached from their meaning, and the entire body of this knowledge began to take on an air of unreality. This experience was not doubt as such, because I still knew and trusted Jesus as risen Lord. But I stopped being able to 'attach' theological and biblical words to whatever they were supposed to describe, a bit like when you repeat some word too much and it just becomes a sound. I was lost among words. The whole body of my theological knowledge seemed as if it were in danger of toppling under its own weight or as if it might somehow come adrift from me and sail off on its own into the blue.

That strange experience vanished as mysteriously as it came. I was very aware of it at the time. But meanwhile, I remained obtusely unaware of the foolishness I sometimes inflicted upon others. Before entering theological college, my friends and I would laugh at those who had what we mockingly called 'curates' disease'; but then I caught it. I harangued people with my knowledge. I grew impatient when they didn't know what I now found obvious. I assaulted groups with theological jargon that made no sense within their discourse. I sneered derisively at theological opponents. In my most extravagant detachments of thought from reality, I would give 'magnificent' sermons which others simply endured with steely determination and unbelievable grace. Perhaps these occupational hazards never quite leave us: there remain some days when the only real change is that I do them as an older fool.

My experience is a glimpse of the way theology can be a dangerous business, both for the one who studies it and for those who have to put up with them. Thankfully though, it turns out that others have known its dangers before us. C.S. Lewis, although not a theologian himself, once addressed some theology students about his role as a Christian apologist. This activity enabled him to warn them of some dangerous moments they should expect for themselves:

> I have found that there is nothing more dangerous to one's own faith than the work of an apologist. No doctrine of that Faith seems to me so spectral, so unreal as one that I have just successfully defended in a public debate. For a moment, you see, it has seemed to rest on oneself: as a result, when you go away from that debate, it seems no stronger than that weak pillar.[2]

In Lewis's moment of unreality, the whole business of faith seemed just to be ensconced inside his head. He was lost among words. It reminded me a little of that experience of unreality I once had and that many others have when introducing others to Christ. The experience is magnified by the modern atheist's argument that theology *in toto* is an imaginary human construct, and that in such moments we are glimpsing 'reality'. (In fact such moments are not unique to theological study. We can temporarily 'lose our grip' on anything we look at closely enough, like the medical student who believes she is on the brink of death simply because she now knows how her body works; or like the budding quantum physicist who begins to doubt whether he can really be the discrete entity we call a 'person'; or like the philosophy student who begins to doubt where anything can actually be *known*.) But Lewis goes on to report another reality:

---

2. C.S. Lewis, 'Christian Apologetics' in *Undeceptions*, ed. Walter Hooper (London: Geoffrey Bles, 1971), p. 76.

That is why we apologists take our lives in our hands and can be saved only by falling back continually from the web of our own arguments, as from our intellectual counters, into the Reality – from Christian apologetics into Christ Himself. That also is why we need one another's continual help – *oremus pro invincem*. ('Let us pray for each other.')[3]

Lewis's dual-pronged counterattack on theology's dangers forms two major themes of this book – firstly, that we must observe and protect our affectionate attachment to Christ; and secondly, that our participation in a loving community of others is integral to the project. I will focus on just one of these for a moment: the matter of affectionate attachment to Christ.

The nineteenth-century Danish philosopher and Christian, Søren Kierkegaard, has a moment of wonderful satire against the theologians of his day. He pictures a coastal road running north from Copenhagen, called Strandvej (and pronounced 'Strath-vie'), which passes through Dyrehaven (pronounced 'Durhahn'), a large wood with many deer. This is the main route to Bakken, where there was a large amusement park. It was a popular Sunday destination for the citizens of Copenhagen.

To me the learned theological world seems like the Strandvej on a Sunday afternoon in the season when everybody goes to Bakken in Dyrehaven: they tear past each other, yell and scream, laugh and make fun of each other, drive their horses to death, overturn, and are run over. Finally, when they reach Bakken covered with dust and out of breath – well, they look at each other – and go home.[4]

---

3. Ibid. p. 76.

4. Kierkegaard, *Letters*, Letter 3; in Søren Kierkegaard, *Either-Or (Part I),* tr. Howard V. Hong and Edna H. Hong, Kierkegaard's Writings, vol. III (Princeton NJ: Princeton University Press, 1987), p. 458.

That is, they have no idea of how, finally, to enjoy the park. By 'enjoying the park' Kierkegaard wants us to see that we have completely missed the point of theology if we are not 'attached' to Jesus in a complex of obedience and loving affection. In a variety of guises, the burden of Kierkegaard's point will be made and remade by the theologians in this volume. 'There is no mistake more terrible than to suppose that activity in Christian work can take the place of depth of Christian affections', says B.B. Warfield.[5]

However some students of theology, having read this far, will already be alarmed. For in our more lucid moments of honesty, we realise that 'affectionate attachment' cannot simply be switched on when it seems to be absent. For frail and wayward beings such as ourselves, the task is beyond us. The wrong kind of talk about 'proper Christian affections' can drift into the heresy of Pelagius, as if we can simply buck ourselves up into the right kind of love for Jesus, and empower ourselves for faithful ministry by the force of a committed will.

We might be reminded of 2 Timothy 2:15, which some translations render as 'do your best to present yourself to God as one approved' [ESV]. 'Doing my best', 'presenting myself' and 'being approved' are usually associated with performance-based recognition – and if *that* is the task of the ambassador of God's grace, then the future for the theological student or worker is only sad. The news of God's grace is now for others only; for us, only merit and measurable performance is left as we toil to 'do our best'. After all, who can ever really 'do their best'? We so regularly fall short of it; and if that performance must *also* include switching on an absent love by will-power, then we shall surely be lost in despair.

---

5. Benjamin B. Warfield, 'The Religious Life of Theological Students', in *Selected Shorter Writings of Benjamin B. Warfield – I*, ed. John E. Meeter (Nutley, N.J.: Presbyterian and Reformed, 1970), p. 424.

But according to the logic of Scripture, people in ministry are as reliant upon the grace of God as anyone else. Charles Spurgeon describes a striking moment when he recognised this reliance:

> I was riding home, very weary with a long week's work, when there came to my mind this text: 'My grace is sufficient for thee' [2 Cor. 12:9 KJV]: but it came with the emphasis laid upon two words: '*My* grace is sufficient for *thee.*' My soul said, 'Doubtless it is. Surely the grace of the infinite God is more than sufficient for such a mere insect as I am', and I laughed, and laughed again, to think how far the supply exceeded all my needs. It seemed to me as though I were a little fish in the sea, and in my thirst I said, 'Alas, I shall drink up the ocean'. Then the Father of the waters lifted up his head sublime, and smilingly replied, 'Little fish, the boundless main is sufficient for thee.'[6]

In fact, the same logic is at work in 2 Timothy 2:15, for as Paul says elsewhere 'it is not the one who commends himself who is approved, but the one whom the Lord commends' [2 Cor. 10:17–18]. The 'workman' remains saved only 'in Christ Jesus' [2 Tim. 2:10], and the sense in which he is 'approved' (or better, 'proven') is the result of having navigated various trials [cf. 2 Cor. 13:7].

Every Christian experiences times when it is harder to trust and love Christ, and so also do theological students, scholars and ministers. The translators of the New Jerusalem Bible are in this case closer to the mark: 'Make every effort to present yourself before God as a proven worker who has no need to be ashamed, but who keeps the message of truth on

---

6. Charles Haddon Spurgeon, *Lectures to my Students: Second Series* (New York: Robert Carter and Sons, 1889), pp. 29-30; online: http://www.archive. org/details/lecturestomystud1889spur (accessed 28th May, 2009).

a straight path.' There are active verbs here, but they are not merely the verbs of a strong, determined will. They describe an active *response* made by the *already-saved* as they meet the enemies of that salvation. Safe 'in Christ', we gradually discover new 'in Christ' reactions to such enemies.

The people in this volume have undergone the trials of theological study before us. They have gradually discovered how to avoid getting lost among words, while studying the Word. We have included both contemporary scholars ('Voices Present'), and respected figures from previous generations ('Voices Past').

That all are men deserves some comment. We simply selected those who have helped us to study theology well. Our selection could be read as an artefact of the majority leadership by men in theology past and present, but I would press further and suggest that the book serendipitously celebrates the work of Jesus Christ among its flawed and limited male authors. Jesus has enabled in them the kinds of humility, care, and love that starkly contrast the regular perversions of masculinity seen elsewhere. We want the book to benefit everyone, for the human and divine themes raised by these men affect everyone. The genius of being 'in Christ' together is that our fellowship can extend across difference; and may some sisters one day showcase whatever has gone unmentioned in the experience and outlook of these men.

Not everything said by these older theologians is without flaw. They sometimes overstress the responsibilities of the theological student, and could have pointed again to the loving kindness of God and the work of his Spirit in frail flesh. Sometimes they need to note that making mistakes and blundering along false trails can be made safe by the enormity of God's redeeming work in Christ, and then repaired by the Holy Spirit who resurrects the dead.

But they will point us to many helps given under the providence of God. They will show how experiences of testing, opposition and even alarm are normal and necessary for the growth of a theologian (Augustine, Luther). We will see how moments of organised community worship of Christ are integral to a proper experience of theology (Augustine, Warfield), just as disordered and corrupted 'community' can divert us from Christ (Lewis). They will guide us in remembering how to do what 'normal' Christians do, in prayer, praise and humble dependence upon God (Warfield). They will sound the alarm against those moments when we want to take shelter in the niceties and nuances of theology, while real evils need to be named and boldly denounced (Bonhoeffer). They will remind us that we remain very, very human, and always rely completely upon the grace of God (Augustine, Spurgeon).

We are also greatly indebted to the contemporary theologians who have kindly contributed to this volume. Each knows and loves the Lord Jesus. Each has been tried by theology. They have experienced its dangerous business.

John Woodhouse surveys the 'realities' of theological college – not the regular daily realities of elective choices, scheduling and amenities – but a vision of what we *really* do in that place, and who we *really* are. Our purpose at such a college is *to know and love God*, and to do so as a loving community. Any lesser view of this time in our lives can only diminish it.

Don Carson observes the manifold risks of studying the Bible. This unparalleled holy collection draws many into theological study. Yet next to its radiance, self-deceptions lurk in shadows unseen. So Carson shows us how to study it with humility. We are alerted to the dangers of Scriptural manipulation and of pride; we consider what level of work is appropriate to its study; we learn how to know its integrity, and how it shapes our own integrity. Carson also includes some useful 'tips' for those who will have a ministry of writing.

Carl Trueman wryly observes – in stark contrast to the high-stakes business of biblical and theological study – that church history does not seem very 'dangerous' at all, largely because most consider it irrelevant. But as he unfolds the risks of simplistic hagiography, and of the extreme historicism that has emerged in reaction to it, we also begin to learn the proper purposes and practices of this discipline.

Gerald Bray dives into the difficulties of studying systematic theology. He alerts us to the dangers of abstraction: that we can simply become lost in its ideas. He alerts us to the danger of apostasy: that many theologians invent something they call 'theology', but which has nothing to do with God. But despite these problems we begin to see that systematic theology has its roots in God, that pastors cannot afford to avoid it even when it is hard, and that it is possible to integrate systematic theology's 'abstractness' with a very personal knowledge and love of God.

Dennis Hollinger points to the way the study of ethics can raise a spectre of moral relativism, or the siren call and burden of legalism, and the disorientation of having our practices and our very identity confronted at our core. But he goes on to show how knowing the Triune God and the Christian worldview leads us out of this maze.

These friends shed some light on our psychology as we engage in theological study; but they do not stop there. In each case, they also give a bird's-eye overview of the deeper logic of their discipline, and of how much it will enable a pastor. They know what it is to experience the dangerous trials of theology, finally to emerge by the loving kindness of God as 'a proven worker who has no need to be ashamed, but who keeps the message of truth on a straight path.' For students struggling blindly through curricula set by others, this news from those a little further down the road gives hope that the road is worth travelling.

We do get lost among theology's words. But Brian Rosner's *Afterword* shows where the Bible's theology leaves us: lost for words, in praise of God.

Andrew Cameron (with Brian Rosner)
Moore Theological College,
Sydney, October 2009

Part I

VOICES PAST

I

Time out to Pray, Read and Weep

Augustine

Augustine (354–430), the fourth-century Bishop of Hippo, stands like Everest among Western theologians. Every serious Christian thinker must take Augustine's thought into account, and his understanding of the Bible still shapes and teaches us today.

But it was not always so. Converted in 386 from a background in pagan philosophy, his early writings betray a shallow knowledge of Scripture. Aware of this problem, and since there was no such thing as a theological seminary, Augustine tried to form a small community of intellectual Christians for the study of the Bible. However, events quickly overtook him.

On a trip back to his homeland he was snapped up by Valerius, the elderly Bishop of Hippo, who urgently needed someone to help him pastor this remote North African province. Augustine desperately wanted to avoid ordination, but was pressured so much by others that he gave in. On the day of his ordination to the priesthood, he wept in open distress. Onlookers thought it obvious that he wept at not receiving the 'top job' of bishop. But Augustine explained later that it was quite the opposite: he wept at his terrible unreadiness even to be a priest.

This letter[1] is addressed to Valerius and was written after Augustine has been in ministry for a short time. He has begun to see how easy it is to do ministry very badly, while being loved by everyone for all the wrong reasons. No longer does he sneer from his armchair at weaknesses in other ministers (or 'sailors', as he calls them); for now, he is acutely aware of his own shortcomings. He begs Valerius for time to 'search through all the remedies' available to him in Scripture.

Modern theological study can often seem like a pointless delay. Or, we may suspiciously regard it as merely a means to control and frustrate those who simply want to tell people about Christ and plant churches.

Augustine's experience suggests otherwise. His desperation highlights the great value of time out *to learn orderly ministry within a righteous life and death – and so that the Lord never asks the question Augustine most fears to hear: 'How do you allege that you had no time to learn how to cultivate my field?'*

To my lord Bishop Valerius, most blessed and venerable, my father most warmly cherished with true love in the sight of the Lord: Augustine, presbyter, sends greeting in the Lord.

Above everything else I ask you to consider this: during our life on earth, and especially in our own day, nothing is easier, pleasanter and more likely to win people's respect than the office of bishop or priest or deacon, if it is performed negligently and with a view to securing their approval; but

---

1. The text is mainly Leinenweber's translation, with some additions for completeness from the older Cunningham translation, and with some editing of both for clarity. References to some biblical allusions have also been added. Augustine, *Letters of Saint Augustine*, tr. John Leinenweber (Liguori, MO: Triumph Books, 1992), pp. 27-9; Augustine, 'Letter XXI', tr. J.G. Cunningham, in *A Select library of the Nicene and post-Nicene fathers of the Christian Church*, ed. Philip Schaff, vol. I (Grand Rapids: Eerdmans, 1988; originally published New York, 1886).

in God's sight there is nothing more sorrowful, miserable, and deserving of condemnation. Again, there is nothing in this present life, and especially now, more difficult, toilsome and perilous than these offices if they are carried out in the way our Lord commands; but, at the same time, nothing is more blessed in God's sight [1 Cor. 3:11f.; 2 Tim. 3:12].

But this 'way our Lord commands' I failed to learn either as a boy or young man; and when I had started to learn it, I was compelled because of my sins (this is the only way I can explain it) to take the second place in your diocese – to help guide the boat, without knowing how to handle an oar!

I know it was the Lord's will to correct me in this way. I was presuming to point out to many sailors their faults, as if I were better and more learned than they, before I had experience in their work. After I was sent in among them I began to feel how rash my fault-finding had been; though even before this experience I had judged their ministry to be a very dangerous one. (That is why I was so troubled at the time of my ordination as priest. Many people noticed this, but they didn't know the cause of my distress. They did what they could to console me, but their words didn't apply to my trouble even though their intention was good.)

But now I have wider and deeper experience in these things than I had when I used to ponder them. I haven't discovered any new waves or storms, nothing I didn't know before, or hadn't heard or read or thought of. But at that time I had no idea of my own skill or strength to avoid them or to put up with them – which I thought were of some value! But the Lord has laughed at me; he has revealed me to myself by means of these experiences.

Now, it may be that God has done this not in judgment but in mercy. At least that is my hope. Now that I know my weakness, I feel I must search through all the remedies his Scriptures contain and give myself to prayer and reading, so that my soul may be given enough strength for its responsible work. This I haven't yet done because I haven't had the time. I was ordained just when I and some others were planning to devote a period of leisure to getting to know the Holy Scriptures. Our intention was to arrange things so that we could be unoccupied for the sake of this occupation. At that time I was still ignorant of how unfit I was for such a work as this one that now worries me and wears me down. But now that I've learned by experience what is required to minister to others God's word and sacrament, I find that I cannot obtain what I know I do not possess. I know that you love both me and the Church to which you intend me to minister, unqualified as I am. You think me qualified; I know myself better, but I wouldn't have come to know myself if experience hadn't taught me.

Perhaps you'll answer that you want to know what is lacking in my education in the faith? There are so many things. I could more easily say what I have, than what I want to have.

This I will say: I know, and unreservedly believe, what concerns my own salvation. My difficulty lies in this: how am I to use this for the salvation of others, not seeking what is helpful to myself but to the many, so that they can be saved? [1 Cor. 10:33] There may be – no, there most certainly are – counsels written in the sacred books which, if a man of God knows and understands them, will enable him to carry out his duties in the Church in a more orderly way; or at least to live among the unrighteous, or to die among them, with a righteous conscience, and not lose that life for which every humble and meek Christian heart longs. But how can this be done except as the Lord tells us [Matt. 7:7], by asking, seeking, and knocking – that is, by praying, reading, and weeping for our sins? It is for this purpose that I have through my brethren made the request for a little time, say until Easter; and this request I now want to renew with this letter.

For what shall I say to the Lord my Judge? [James 3:1] Shall I say, 'I was not able to acquire what I needed, because I was engrossed wholly with the affairs of the Church'? What if he replied 'You wicked servant! ... How do you allege that you had no time to learn how to cultivate my field?' [Matt. 25:26; 1 Cor. 3:9] Tell me, I beg you, what could I reply? Are you willing for me to say, 'Old Valerius is to blame'? 'Believing I had been instructed in all things necessary, he declined to give me permission to learn what I had not acquired.'

Consider all these things, aged Valerius; consider them, I beg you, by the goodness and severity of Christ, by his mercy and judgment, by him who has inspired you with such love for me that I dare not displease you, even when the advantage of my soul is at stake. I therefore appeal to your love and affection for me. Have pity on me and grant me the time which I have asked for the purpose for which I have asked it. Help me with your prayers, that my absence may bear fruit for the Church of Christ and may profit my brethren and fellow-servants. I know that the Lord will not despise your love interceding for me, especially in such a cause as this. Perhaps he will restore me to you within a period shorter than I have craved, thoroughly furnished for his service by the profitable counsels of his written word.

2

Experience Makes the Theologian

Martin Luther

Little did Martin Luther (1483–1546) know that his discoveries in Romans, Galatians and the Psalms in the 1510s would trigger the earthquake in continental theology that we now call 'the Reformation'. In those tumultuous decades of the sixteenth-century, Luther lived through lows that he could hardly bear. He is justly famous for asserting the principle of sola scriptura, where the Bible is able to convey all we need for faith and salvation. But at his lowest, he also learned that if theologians are to become 'good' theologians, they must also experience the gospel's comfort to broken sinners. His writing has a medieval tone that can be difficult to understand, so we have selected some excerpts[1] and added a few explanatory notes.

Martin Luther's comment on the way to be a theologian is cryptic at first sight:

> Teachers of law can humble their students when the students try to put on airs about their learning, because they have a court and get practical experience. On the other hand, we can't humble our students because we have no practical exercises. Yet experience alone makes the theologian.[2]

---

1. The editors are thankful to Rev. Dr Mark Thompson for directing us to these selections. For an excellent commentary, see John Kleinig, 'Oratio, Meditatio, Tentatio: What Makes a Theologian?', *Concordia Theological Quarterly* 66 no. 3 (2002); online: http://www.ctsfw.edu/library/files/ pb/896 (accessed 14th February, 2007).

2. Helmut T. Lehmann and Theodore G. Tappert, eds., *Luther's Works: Table Talk*, vol. 54, (Philadelphia: Fortress, 1967), p. 7.

In other words, it would be best for a student to be put through 'humbling experiences'; but teachers of theology should not really treat people in that way! When later he expands upon this comment, we begin to see why such a 'humbling' would help students of theology. Trials over which we have no control enable us to discover the proper use of theology to console us. We also discover the way theology's misuse only deepens our despair:

I didn't learn my theology all at once. I had to ponder over it ever more deeply, and my spiritual trials were of help to me in this, for one does not learn anything without practice. This is what the spiritualists and sects lack. They don't have the right adversary, the devil. He would teach them well. None of the arts can be learned without practice. What kind of physician would that be who stayed in school all the time? When he finally puts his medicine to use and deals more and more with nature, he will come to see that he hasn't as yet mastered the art. Why shouldn't this be so in the case of the Holy Scriptures, too, where God has provided a different adversary? It is therefore the greatest gift (of God) to have a text and to be able to say, 'This is right. I know it.' People think that they can know everything by simply listening to a sermon. Zwingli also made the mistake of thinking that he knew everything, that theology is an easy art. But I know that I have yet to comprehend the Lord's Prayer. No one can be learned without practice. The peasant put it well: Armour is fine for a man who knows how to use it. To be sure, the Holy Scriptures are sufficient in themselves, but God grant that I find the right text. For when Satan disputes with me whether God is gracious to me, I dare not quote the passage, 'He who loves God will inherit the kingdom of God,' [cf. 1 Cor. 2:9] because Satan will at once object, 'But you have not loved God!' Nor can I oppose this on the ground that I am a diligent reader (of the Scriptures) and a preacher. The shoe doesn't fit. I should say, rather, that Jesus Christ died for me and should cite the article (of the Creed) concerning forgiveness of sin. That will do it![3]

The following extended statement outlines 'a correct way of studying theology'. *We can make no real progress in Christian knowledge if it is not appropriated to ourselves in prayer and repeated oral meditation. (His recommended practice of repeatedly reading Scripture aloud seems odd to us – but it was once considered the proper way to read seriously.) He ends by reworking the concept of experience-based learning through trials. His approach is summed up in a famous triad that no theologian can be without:* oratio, meditatio *and* tentatio; *that is, prayer, meditation – and temptation!*

I want to point out to you a correct way of studying theology, for I have had practice in that. If you keep to it, you will become so learned that you yourself could (if it were necessary) write books just as good as those of the fathers and councils, even as I (in God) dare to presume and boast, without arrogance and lying, that in the matter of writing books I do not stand much behind some of the fathers. Of my life I can by no means make the same boast. This is the way taught by holy King David (and doubtlessly used also by all the patriarchs and prophets) in Psalm 119. There you will find three rules, amply presented throughout the whole Psalm. They are *oratio, meditatio, tentatio* [prayer, meditation, temptation].

Firstly, you should know that the Holy Scriptures constitute a book which turns the wisdom of all other books into foolishness, because not one teaches about eternal life except this one alone. Therefore you should straightway despair of your reason and understanding. With them you will not attain eternal life, but, on the contrary, your presumptuousness will plunge you and others with you out of heaven (as happened to Lucifer) into the abyss of hell. But kneel down in your little room

---

3.   Ibid. pp. 50-1.

[Matt. 6:6] and pray to God with real humility and earnestness, that he through his dear Son may give you his Holy Spirit, who will enlighten you, lead you, and give you understanding.

Thus you see how David keeps praying in the above-mentioned Psalm, 'Teach me, Lord, instruct me, lead me, show me', and many more words like these. Although he well knew and daily heard and read the text of Moses and other books besides, still he wants to lay hold of the real Teacher of the Scriptures himself, so that he may not seize upon them pell-mell with his reason and become his own teacher. For such practice gives rise to factious spirits who allow themselves to nurture the delusion that the Scriptures are subject to them and can be easily grasped with their reason, as if they were [the ancient German fable] Markolf or Aesop's Fables, for which no Holy Spirit and no prayers are needed.

Secondly, you should meditate, that is, not only in your heart, but also externally, by actually repeating and comparing oral speech and literal words of the book, reading and rereading them with diligent attention and reflection, so that you may see what the Holy Spirit means by them. And take care that you do not grow weary or think that you have done enough when you have read, heard, and spoken them once or twice, and that you then have complete understanding. You will never be a particularly good theologian if you do that, for you will be like untimely fruit which falls to the ground before it is half ripe.

Thus you see in this same Psalm how David constantly boasts that he will talk, meditate, speak, sing, hear, read, by day and night and always, about nothing except God's word and commandments. For God will not give you his Spirit without the external word; so take your cue from that. His command to write, preach, read, hear, sing, speak, etc., outwardly was not given in vain.

Thirdly, there is *tentatio, Anfechtung*. This is the touchstone which teaches you not only to know and understand, but also to experience how right, how true, how sweet, how lovely, how mighty, how comforting God's word is, wisdom beyond all wisdom.

Thus you see how David, in the Psalm mentioned, complains so often about all kinds of enemies, arrogant princes or tyrants, false spirits and factions, whom he must tolerate because he meditates, that is, because he is occupied with God's word (as has been said) in all manner of ways. For as soon as God's word takes root and grows in you, the devil will harry you, and will make a real doctor of you, and by his assaults will teach you to seek and love God's word. I myself (if you will permit me, mere mouse-dirt, to be mingled with pepper) am deeply indebted to my papists that through the devil's raging they have beaten, oppressed, and distressed me so much. That is to say, they have made a fairly good theologian of me, which I would not have become otherwise. And I heartily grant them what they have won in return for making this of me – honour, victory, and triumph – for that's the way they wanted it.

There now, with that you have David's rules. If you study hard in accord with his example, then you will also sing and boast with him in the Psalm, 'The law of thy mouth is better to me than thousands of gold and silver pieces' [Ps. 119:72 RSV]. Also, 'Thy commandment makes me wiser than my enemies, for it is ever with me. I have more understanding than all my teachers, for thy testimonies are my meditation. I understand more than the aged, for I keep thy precepts,' etc. [Ps. 119:98-100 RSV]. And it will be your experience that the books of the fathers will taste stale and putrid to you in comparison. You will not only despise the books written by adversaries, but the longer you write and teach the less you will be pleased with yourself. When you have reached this point, then do not be afraid to hope that you have begun to become a real theologian, who can teach not only the young and imperfect Christians, but also the maturing and perfect ones. For indeed, Christ's church has all kinds of Christians in it who are young, old, weak, sick, healthy, strong, energetic, lazy, simple, wise, etc.

If, however, you feel and are inclined to think you have made it, flattering yourself with your own little books, teaching, or writing, because you have done it beautifully and preached excellently; if you are highly pleased when someone praises you in the presence of others; if you perhaps look for praise, and would sulk or quit what you are doing if you did not get it – if you are of that stripe, dear friend, then take yourself by the ears, and if you do this in the right way you will find a beautiful pair of big, long, shaggy donkey ears. Then do not spare any expense! Decorate them with golden bells, so that people will be able to hear you wherever you go, point their fingers at you, and say, 'See, See! There goes that clever beast, who can write such exquisite books and preach so remarkably well.' That very moment you will be blessed and blessed beyond measure in the kingdom of heaven. Yes, in that heaven where hellfire is ready for the devil and his angels. To sum up: Let us be proud and seek honour in the places where we can. But in this book the honour is God's alone, as it is said. 'God opposes the proud, but gives grace to the humble' [1 Pet. 5:5 RSV]; to whom be glory, world without end, Amen.[4]

These selections have highlighted Luther's understanding of the way God shapes a real theologian through the experience of living the gospel, and the aching joy of sins forgiven. Luther's spectacular claim should have the last word:

It is not understanding, reading or speculation, but living – no, dying and being damned – that makes a theologian.[5]

---

4. Jaroslav Pelikan, *et al.*, eds., *Luther's Works: Career of the Reformer IV*, vol. 34, (Philadelphia: Muhlenberg, 1960), pp. 285-8.

5. Luther, Second Series of Psalms Lectures (*Operationes in Psalmnos*) (1519–21) *WA* 5, 163 pp. 28-9.

3

Frailty and the Grace of God

Charles Haddon Spurgeon

Charles Haddon Spurgeon (1834–1892), the famous Baptist preacher at the Metropolitan Tabernacle at London's Elephant and Castle, also founded The Pastor's College *in 1857. This volume could not be complete without some reference to* Lectures To My Students,[1] *a collection of talks addressing many aspects of students' and pastors' lives.*

Several aspects of Spurgeon's approach are worth noting. His genius for metaphor will strike you first. Spurgeon had an amazing capacity to string pungent images together. Each metaphor could be 'risky' on its own, but his commanding theological awareness meant that he could employ several such metaphors with an overall 'self-

---

1. Only some abridged sections of some lectures have been reproduced here. As always, there is no substitute for reading the original: Charles Haddon Spurgeon, *Lectures to my Students: First Series* (London: Passmore and Alabaster, 1875); online: http://www.archive.org/details/lecturestomystu00spuruoft (accessed 21st February, 2007); Spurgeon, *Lectures: Second Series* (cited in 'Foreword', above); and Charles Haddon Spurgeon, *Lectures to My Students: Complete and Unabridged; New Edition containing Selected Lectures from Series 1, 2 and 3* (Grand Rapids: Ministry Resources Library/Zondervan, 1989; originally published by Marshall, Morgan and Scott Ltd, 1954). The name of each lecture is given in brackets at each heading, and the order in which lectures have been reproduced is not the order in which they were given. Some minor amendments have been made; small deletions have not been indicated; and ellipsis only indicates where major sections are omitted.

correcting' effect. This metaphorical style may amuse us at first, but we should take care not to lose the profound importance of each main point.

Second, Spurgeon intentionally blurs the distinction between 'student', 'preacher' and 'minister', since he believes that no student of theology should be such a student without a firm intention and clear ability to go on as a minister of the gospel to others.

Third, although Spurgeon acutely observes the frailties of human nature, he has unbounded confidence in the goodness and graciousness of God to assist us through these difficulties.

Preparation ('The call to ministry'). ... From someone or other I heard in conversation of a plan adopted by Matthew Wilks, for examining a young man who wanted to be a missionary; the drift, if not the detail of the test, commends itself to my judgment though not to my taste.

The young man desired to go to India as a missionary in connection with the London Missionary Society. Mr Wilks was appointed to consider his fitness for such a post. He wrote to the young man, and told him to call upon him at six o'clock the next morning. The brother lived many miles off but he was at the house at six o'clock punctually.

Mr Wilks did not, however, enter the room until hours after. The brother waited wonderingly, but patiently. At last, Mr Wilks arrived, and addressed the candidate thus, in his usual nasal tones, 'Well, young man, so you want to be a missionary?'

'Yes, Sir.'

'Do you love the Lord Jesus Christ?'

'Yes, Sir, I hope I do.'

'And have you had any education?'

'Yes, Sir, a little.'

'Well, now, we'll try you; can you spell "cat"?'

The young man looked confused, and hardly knew how to answer so preposterous a question. His mind evidently halted between indignation and submission, but in a moment he replied steadily, 'C, A, T, cat.'

'Very good,' said Mr Wilks; 'now, can you spell "dog"?' Our young martyr hesitated, but Mr Wilks said in his coolest manner, 'Oh, never mind; don't be bashful; you spelt the other word so well that I should think you will be able to spell this: high as the attainment is, it is not so elevated but what you might do it without blushing.'

The youthful Job replied, 'D, O, G, dog.'

'Well, that is right; I see you will do in your spelling, and now for your arithmetic; how many are twice two?' It is a wonder that Mr Wilks did not receive 'twice two' after the fashion of muscular Christianity, but the patient youth gave the right reply and was dismissed.

Matthew Wilks at the committee meeting said, 'I cordially recommend that young man; his testimonials and character I have duly examined, and besides that, I have given him a rare personal trial such as few could bear. I tried his self-denial, he was up in the morning early; I tried his temper, and I tried his humility; he can spell cat and dog, and can tell that twice two make four, and he will do for a missionary exceedingly well.'

Now what the old gentleman is thus said to have done with exceedingly bad taste, we may with much propriety do with ourselves. We must try whether we can endure brow-beating, weariness, slander, jeering and hardship; and whether we can be made the off-scouring of all things, and be treated as nothing for Christ's sake. If we can endure all these, we have some of those points which indicate the possession of the rare qualities which should meet in a true servant of the Lord Jesus

Christ. I gravely question whether some of us will find our vessels, when far out at sea, to be quite so seaworthy as we think them. O my brethren, make sure work of it while you are yet in this retreat; and diligently labour to fit yourselves for your high calling. You will have trials enough, and woe to you if you do not go forth armed from head to foot with armour of proof. You will have to run with horsemen; let not the footmen weary you while in your preliminary studies. The devil is abroad, and with him are many. Prove your own selves, and may the Lord prepare you for the crucible and the furnace which assuredly await you.

Your tribulation may not in all respects be so severe as that of Paul and his companions, but you must be ready for a like ordeal. Let me read you his memorable words, and let me entreat you to pray, while you hear them, that the Holy Ghost may strengthen you for all that lies before you.

> Giving no offence in any thing, that the ministry be not blamed: but in all things approving ourselves as the ministers of God, in much patience, in afflictions, in necessities, in distresses, in stripes, in imprisonments, in tumults, in labours, in watchings, in fastings; by pureness, by knowledge, by long-suffering, by kindness, by the Holy Ghost, by love unfeigned, by the word of truth, by the power of God, by the armour of righteousness on the right hand and on the left, by honour and dishonour, by evil report and good report: as deceivers, and yet true; as unknown, and yet well known; as dying, and, behold, we live; as chastened, and not killed; as sorrowful, yet always rejoicing; as poor, yet making many rich; as having nothing, and yet possessing all things. [2 Cor. 6:3-10, KJV]

Self-awareness ('The Minister's Self-watch').

> 'Take heed unto thyself, and unto the doctrine.'
> [1 Tim. 4:16, KJV]

Every workman knows the necessity of keeping his tools in a good state of repair, for 'if the iron be blunt, and he do not whet the edge, then must he put to more strength.' If the workman lose the edge from his adze, he knows that there will be a greater draught upon his energies, or his work will be badly done. Michelangelo, the elect of the fine arts, understood so well the importance of his tools, that he always made his own brushes with his own hands, and in this he gives us an illustration of the God of grace, who with special care fashions for himself all true ministers.

We are, in a certain sense, our own tools, and therefore must keep ourselves in order. If I want to preach the gospel, I can only use my own voice; therefore I must train my vocal powers. I can only think with my own brains, and feel with my own heart, and therefore I must educate my intellectual and emotional faculties. I can only weep and agonise for souls in my own renewed nature, therefore must I watchfully maintain the tenderness which was in Christ Jesus.

It will be in vain for me to stock my library, or organise societies, or project schemes, if I neglect the culture of myself; for books, and agencies, and systems, are only remotely the instruments of my holy calling; my own spirit, soul, and body, are my nearest machinery for sacred service; my spiritual faculties, and my inner life, are my battle-axe and weapons of war. M'Cheyne,[2] writing to a ministerial friend

---

2.   Spurgeon is referring to the famous Scottish Presbyterian preacher, Robert Murray McCheyne (1813–1843)

who was travelling with a view to perfecting himself in the German tongue, used language identical with our own:

> I know you will apply hard to German, but do not forget the culture of the inner man – I mean of the heart. How diligently the cavalry officer keeps his sabre clean and sharp; every stain he rubs off with the greatest care. Remember you are God's sword, his instrument I trust, a chosen vessel unto him to bear his name. In great measure, according to the purity and perfection of the instrument, will be the success. It is not great talents God blesses so much as likeness to Jesus. A holy minister is an awful weapon in the hand of God.[3]

That a teacher of the gospel should first be a partaker of it is a simple truth, but at the same time a rule of the most weighty importance. The world is full of counterfeits, and swarms with panderers to carnal self-conceit, who gather around a minister as vultures around a carcass. Our own hearts are deceitful, so that truth lies not on the surface, but must be drawn up from the deepest well. We must search ourselves very anxiously and very thoroughly, lest by any means after having preached to others we ourselves should be castaways. How horrible to be a preacher of the gospel and yet to be unconverted! Let each man here whisper to his own inmost soul, 'What a dreadful thing it will be for me if I should be ignorant of the power of the truth which I am preparing to proclaim!'

Unconverted ministry involves the most unnatural relationships. A graceless pastor is a blind man elected to

---

3. Andrew A. Bonar (ed.), *Memoir and Remains of the Rev. Robert Murray McCheyne* (Philadelphia, Presbyterian Board of Publications, c. 1844), p. 258; online:http://www.archive.org/details/robertmurraymcch00bonauoft (accessed 2nd December, 2009).

a professorship of optics, philosophising upon light and vision, discoursing upon and distinguishing to others the nice shades and delicate blendings of the prismatic colours, while he himself is absolutely in the dark! He is a dumb man elevated to the chair of music; a deaf man fluent upon symphonies and harmonies! He is a mole professing to educate eaglets; a limpet elected to preside over angels. To such a relationship one might apply the most absurd and grotesque metaphors, except that the subject is too solemn. It is a dreadful position for a man to stand in, for he has undertaken a work for which he is totally, wholly, and altogether unqualified, but from the responsibilities of which this unfitness will not screen him, because he wilfully incurred them. Whatever his natural gifts, whatever his mental powers may be, he is utterly out of court for spiritual work if he has no spiritual life; and it is his duty to cease the ministerial office till he has received this first and simplest of qualifications for it.

We have all heard the story of the man who preached so well and lived so badly, that when he was in the pulpit everybody said he ought never to come out again, and when he was out of it they all declared he never ought to enter it again. Too many preachers forget to serve God when they are out of the pulpit; their lives are negatively inconsistent. Abhor, dear brethren, the thought of being clockwork ministers who are not alive by abiding grace within, but are wound up by temporary influences; men who are only ministers for the time being, under the stress of the hour of ministering, but cease to be ministers when they descend the pulpit stairs. True ministers are always ministers. Too many preachers are like those sand-toys we buy for our children: you turn the box upside down, and the little acrobat revolves and revolves till the sand is all run down, and then he hangs motionless. So there are some who persevere in the ministrations of truth as long as there is an official necessity for their work, but after that – no salary, no sermon.

It is a horrible thing to be an inconsistent minister ...

Reading and thinking ('To workers with slender apparatus'). *Spurgeon devotes a lecture to students who cannot afford many books. Several helpful suggestions are given; here we reproduce three. Typically, Spurgeon goes well beyond the immediate practical problem to much deeper questions of character.*

... The next rule I shall lay down is, *master those books you have*. Read them thoroughly. Bathe in them until they saturate you. Read and reread them, chew them, and digest them. Let them go into your very self. Peruse a good book several times, and make notes and analyses of it. A student will find that his mental constitution is more affected by one book thoroughly mastered than by twenty books which he has merely skimmed, lapping at them, as the classic proverb puts it, 'as dogs drink of the Nile'. Little learning and much pride come of hasty reading. Books may be piled on the brain till it cannot work. Some men are disabled from thinking by their putting meditation away for the sake of much reading. They gorge themselves with book-matter, and become mentally dyspeptic.

Books *on* the brain cause disease. Get the book *into* the brain, and you will grow. In Disraeli's *Curiosities of Literature* there is an invective of Lucian upon those men who boast of possessing large libraries, which they either never read or never profit by. He begins by comparing such a person to a pilot who has never learned the art of navigation, or a cripple who wears embroidered slippers but cannot stand upright in them. Then he exclaims, 'Why do you buy so many books? You have no hair, and you purchase a comb; you are blind, and you must buy a fine mirror; you are deaf, and you will have the best musical instrument!' – a very well deserved rebuke to those who think that the possession of books will secure them learning. A measure of that temptation happens to us all; for do we not feel wiser after we have spent an hour or two in a bookseller's shop? A man might as well think himself richer for having inspected the vaults of the Bank of England. In reading books let your motto be, 'Much, not many'. Think as well as read, and keep the thinking always proportionate to the reading, and your small library will not be a great misfortune.

... A man who has learned not merely the letter of the Bible, but its inner spirit, will be no mean man, whatever deficiencies he may labour under. You know the old proverb, *'Beware of the man of one book'*. He is a terrible antagonist. A man who has his Bible at his fingers' ends and in his heart's core is a champion in our Israel. You cannot compete with him. You may have an armoury of weapons, but his Scriptural knowledge will overcome you. It is a sword like that of Goliath, of which David said, 'There is none like it'. The gracious William Romaine, I believe, in the latter part of his life, put away all his books and read nothing at all but his Bible. He was a scholarly man, yet he was monopolised by the one Book, and was made mighty by it. If we are driven to do the same by necessity, let us recollect that some have done it by choice, and let us not bemoan our lot, for the Scriptures will be sweeter than honey to our taste, and will make us 'wiser than the ancients'. We shall never be short of holy matter if we are continually studying the inspired volume; nay, it is not only matter that we shall find there, but illustration too. For the Bible is its own best illustrator. If you want anecdote, simile, allegory, or parable, turn to the sacred page. Scriptural truth never looks more lovely than when she is adorned with jewels from her own treasury. I have lately been reading the Books of the Kings and the Chronicles, and I have become enamoured of them; they are as full of divine instruction as the Psalms or Prophets, if read with opened eyes. I think it was Ambrose who used to say, 'I adore the infinity of Scripture'. I hear that same voice which sounded in the ears of Augustine, concerning the Book of God, '*Tolle, lege*', 'Take, read'. It may be you will dwell in retirement in some village, where you will find no one to converse with who is above your own level, and where you will meet with very few books worth your reading; then read and meditate in the law of the Lord both day and night, and you shall be 'as a tree planted by the rivers of water'. Make the Bible the man of your right hand, the companion of every hour, and you will have little reason to lament your slender equipment in inferior things.

... Moreover, however scant your libraries, *you can study yourself.* This is a mysterious volume, the major part of which you have not read. If any man thinks that he knows himself thoroughly, he deceives himself; for the most difficult book you will ever read is your own heart. I said to a doubter the other day, who seemed to be wandering in a maze, 'Well, really I cannot understand you but I am not vexed, for I never could understand myself'; and I certainly meant what I said. Watch the twists and turns and singularities of your own mind, and the strangeness of your own experience; the depravity of your heart, and the work of divine grace; your tendency to sin, and your capacity for holiness; how akin you are to a devil, and yet how allied to God himself! Note how wisely you can act when taught of God, and how foolishly you behave when left to yourself. You will find the study of your heart to be of immense importance to you as a watcher over the souls of others. A man's own experience should be to him the laboratory in which he tests the medicines which he prescribes for others. Even your own faults and failures will instruct you if you bring them to the Lord. Absolutely sinless men would be unable to sympathise with imperfect men and women. Study the Lord's dealings with your own souls, and you will know more of his ways with others.

Prayer ('The Preacher's Private Prayer'). ... While the unformed minister is revolving upon the wheel of preparation, prayer is the tool of the great potter by which he moulds vessel. All our libraries and studies are mere emptiness compared with our closets. We grow, we wax mighty, we prevail in private prayer.

Your prayers will be your ablest assistants *while your discourses are yet upon the anvil*. While other men, like Esau, are hunting for their portion, you, by the aid of prayer, will find the savoury meat near at home, and may say in truth what Jacob said so falsely, 'The Lord brought it to me.' If you can dip your pens into your hearts, appealing in earnestness to the Lord, you will write well; and if you can gather your matter on your knees at the gate of heaven, you will not fail to speak well. Prayer, as a mental exercise, will bring many subjects before the mind, and so help in the selection of a topic, while as a high spiritual engagement it will cleanse your inner eye that you may see truth in the light of God. Texts will often refuse to reveal their treasures till you open them with the key of prayer. How wonderfully were the books opened to Daniel when he was in supplication! How much Peter learned upon the housetop! The closet is the best study. The commentators are good instructors, but the Author Himself is far better, and prayer makes a direct appeal to him and enlists him in our cause. It is a great thing to pray one's self into the spirit and marrow of a text, working into it by sacred feeding thereon, even as the worm bores its way into the kernel of the nut. Prayer supplies a leverage for the uplifting of ponderous truths. One marvels how the stones of Stonehenge could have been set in their places; it is even more to be enquired after whence some men obtained such admirable knowledge of mysterious doctrines: was not prayer the potent machinery which wrought the wonder? Waiting upon God often turns darkness into light. Persevering enquiry at the sacred oracle uplifts the veil and gives grace to look into the deep things of God. A certain Puritan divine at a debate was observed frequently to write upon the paper before him; upon others curiously seeking to read his notes, they found nothing upon the page but the words, 'More light, Lord', 'More light, Lord', repeated scores of times: a most suitable prayer for the student of the word when preparing his discourse.

... Prayer will *singularly assist you in the delivery of your sermon*; in fact, nothing can so gloriously fit you to preach as descending fresh from the mount of communion with God to speak with men. None are so able to plead with men as those who have been wrestling with God on their behalf. ... There is no rhetoric like that of the heart, and no school for learning it but the foot of the cross. It were better that you never learned a rule of human oratory, but were full of the power of heaven-born love, than that you should master Quintilian, Cicero and Aristotle, and remain without the apostolic anointing.

... The minister who does not earnestly pray over his work must surely be a vain and conceited man. He acts as if he thought himself sufficient of himself, and therefore needed not to appeal to God. Yet what a baseless pride to conceive that our preaching can ever be in itself so powerful that it can turn men from their sins, and bring them to God without the working of the Holy Ghost. If we are truly humble-minded we shall not venture down to the fight until the Lord of Hosts has clothed us with all power, and said to us, 'Go in this thy might'. The preacher who neglects to pray much must be very careless about his ministry. He cannot have comprehended his calling. He cannot have computed the value of a soul, or estimated the meaning of eternity. He must be a mere official, tempted into a pulpit because the piece of bread which belongs to the priest's office is very necessary to him, or a detestable hypocrite who loves the praise of men, and cares not for the praise of God. He will surely become a mere superficial talker, best approved where grace is least valued and a vain show most admired. He cannot be one of those who plough deep and reap abundant harvests. He is a mere loiterer, not a labourer. As a preacher he has a name to live and is dead. He limps in his life like the lame man in the Proverbs, whose legs were not equal, for his praying is shorter than his preaching.

I am afraid that, more or less, most of us need self-examination as to this matter. If any man here should venture to say that he prays as much as he ought as a student, I should gravely question his statement; and if there be a minister, deacon, or elder present who can say that he believes he is occupied with God in prayer to the full extent to which he might be, I should be pleased to know him. I can only say, that if he can claim this excellence, he leaves me far behind, for I can make no such claim: I wish I could; and I make the confession with no small degree of shamefacedness and confusion, but I am obliged to make it. ...

Depression ('The Minister's fainting fits').
Fits of depression come over the most of us. Usually cheerful as we may be, we must at intervals be cast down. The strong are not always vigorous, the wise not always ready, the brave not always courageous, and the joyous not always happy.

... Knowing by most painful experience what deep depression of spirit means, being visited therewith at seasons by no means few or far between, I thought it might be consolatory to some of my brethren if I gave my thoughts thereon, that younger men might not fancy that some strange thing had happened to them when they became for a season possessed by melancholy; and that sadder men might know that one upon whom the sun has shone right joyously did not always walk in the light.

Spurgeon lists several reasons why people in ministry become depressed:

- *We are human. (Spurgeon quotes the 'wise man' of the Apocrypha, reproduced here in a modern translation:)*

  Hard work was created for everyone, and a heavy yoke is laid on the children of Adam, from the day they come forth from their mother's womb until the day they return to the mother of all the living. Perplexities and fear of heart are theirs, and anxious thought of the day of their death. From the one who sits on a splendid throne to the one who grovels in dust and ashes, from the one who wears purple and a crown to the one who is clothed in burlap, there is anger and envy and trouble and unrest, and fear of death, and fury and strife. And when one rests upon his bed, his sleep at night confuses his mind. He gets little or no rest; he struggles in his sleep as he did by day. He is troubled by the visions of his mind like one who has escaped from the battlefield. At the moment he reaches safety he wakes up, astonished that his fears were groundless. To all creatures, human and animal, but to sinners seven times more, come death and bloodshed and strife and sword, calamities and famine and ruin and plague. [Ecclus./Sir. 40:1-9, NRSV]

- *Physical and mental unwellness:* ... Moreover, most of us are in some way or other unsound physically. Here and there we meet with an old man who could not remember that ever he was laid aside for a day; but the great mass of us labour under some form or other of infirmity, either in body or mind. Certain bodily maladies, especially those connected with the digestive organs, the liver and the spleen, are the fruitful fountains of despondency; and, let a man strive as he may against their influence, there will be hours and circumstances in which they will for a while overcome him. As to mental maladies, is any man altogether sane? Are we not all a little off the balance? Some minds appear to have a gloomy tinge essential to their very individuality. Of them it may be said, 'Melancholy marked them for her own.' These are fine minds withal and ruled by noblest principles, but are most prone to forget the silver lining and to remember only the cloud.

- *The sad nature of our work:* ... Who can bear the weight of souls without sometimes sinking to the dust? Passionate longings after men's conversion, if not fully satisfied (and when are they?) consume the soul with anxiety and disappointment. To see the hopeful turn aside, the godly grow cold, professors abusing their privileges and sinners waxing more bold in sin – are not these sights enough to crush us to the earth?

- *The minister's lonely, unique position:* ... Men of God who rise above their fellows into nearer communion with heavenly things, in their weaker moments feel the lack of human sympathy. Like their Lord in Gethsemane they look in vain for comfort to the disciples sleeping around them; they are shocked at the apathy of their little band of brethren, and return to their secret agony with all the heavier burden pressing upon them because they have found their dearest companions slumbering.

- *Sedentary habits:* ... To sit long in one posture, poring over a book or driving a quill, is in itself a taxing of nature; but add to this a badly ventilated chamber, a body which has long been without muscular exercise and a heart burdened with many cares, and we have all the elements for preparing a seething cauldron of despair, especially in the dim months of fog. Let a man be naturally as blithe as a bird, he will hardly be able to bear up year after year against such a suicidal process: he will make his study a prison and his books the warders of a gaol, while nature lies outside his window calling him to health and beckoning him to joy. He who forgets the humming of the bees among the heather, the cooing of the wood-pigeons in the forest, the song of birds in the woods, the rippling of rills among the rushes, and the sighing of the wind among the pines, needs not wonder if his heart forgets to sing and his soul grows heavy. A day's breathing of fresh air upon the hills or a few hours' ramble in the beech woods' umbrageous calm would sweep the cobwebs out of the brain of scores of our toiling ministers who are now but half alive. A mouthful of sea air or a stiff walk in the wind's face would not give grace to the soul, but it would yield oxygen to the body, which is next best.

- *Depression also strikes at predictable moments (and summarising Spurgeon's other sub-headings, these are: after great success; before great achievements; during extended periods of hard work; after a crushing disappointment; when several troubles have piled up. Or, it can simply have unknown causes. But Spurgeon's advice about how to respond relies completely on the grace of God, who keeps us safe in Christ even at our worst:)*

... By all the castings down of his servants God is glorified, for they are led to magnify him when again he sets them on their feet, and even while prostrate in the dust their faith yields him praise. They speak all the more sweetly of his faithfulness, and are the more firmly established in his love.

The lesson of wisdom is *be not dismayed by soul-trouble*. Count it no strange thing, but a part of ordinary ministerial experience. Should the power of depression be more than ordinary, think not that all is over with your usefulness. Cast not away your confidence, for it hath great recompense of reward. Even if the enemy's foot be on your neck, expect to rise and overthrow him. Cast the burden of the present, along with the sin of the past and the fear of the future, upon the Lord, who forsaketh not his saints. Live by the day – by the hour even.

... Set small store by present rewards; be grateful for earnests by the way, but look for the recompensing joy hereafter. Continue, with double earnestness to serve your Lord when no visible result is before you. Any simpleton can follow the narrow path in the light: faith's rare wisdom enables us to march on in the dark with infallible accuracy, since she places her hand in that of her Great Guide. Between this and heaven there may be rougher weather yet, but it is all provided for by our covenant Head. In nothing let us be turned aside from the path which the divine call has urged us to pursue. Come fair or come foul, the pulpit is our watchtower, and the ministry our warfare; be it ours, when we cannot see the face of our God, to trust under THE SHADOW OF HIS WINGS.

4

The Spiritual Life of Theological Students

Benjamin B. Warfield

Benjamin Breckinridge Warfield (1851–1921) was the great principal of Princeton Seminary from 1887 to 1921. He developed a tradition of Reformed Calvinist thought that still has an immense influence among evangelicals today.

This famous address, The Religious Life of Theological Students,[1] *was first published in 1911. It really needs no introduction, for Warfield had no difficulty in speaking clearly, but a few points are worth noting.*

Modern readers react against the term 'religious', used by Warfield to refer to a person's private practices and to the inner life from which they spring. (This inner life is called the 'heart' in the Bible: those hidden passions, affections, thoughts and motivations that are known only by God and to a lesser extent by us.) The best modern substitute for 'religious life' would be 'spiritual life' (or perhaps 'spirituality'), hence our change of this chapter's title.

Warfield devotes his energy to two main claims. First, the student's task or 'vocation' is to study hard. Students are called to learn with the same diligence that the Lord expects of a Christian at work anywhere.

Second, Warfield insists that a person's spiritual life cannot be sustained solely through this study. Surprisingly for many modern

---

1. For the source of this address see fn. 5 from *Foreword* p .11.

Protestant readers, Warfield vocally argues that a seminary's activities of communal worship are non-negotiable, and act as a bedrock to healthy spirituality.

His claims become quite confronting. Warfield is worried by 'restless activity at the apparent expense of depth of spiritual culture' among students; for there is 'no mistake more terrible than to suppose that activity in Christian work can take the place of depth of Christian affections'. In other words, theological study dangerously tempts us to become unspiritual people.

We invite you to reflect seriously upon Warfield's forcefulness, such as when he holds hearers to evangelical practices of piety that few would consider today (e.g. early-morning winter prayers, or Sunday afternoon Bible lectures). We thoughtlessly tend to reject these as ancient relics. But perhaps a more useful response is to ask: 'what makes me so sure my own practices are better?'

I am asked to speak to you on the religious life of the student of theology. I approach the subject with some trepidation. I think it the most important subject which can engage our thought. You will not suspect me in saying this to be depreciating the importance of the intellectual preparation of the student for the ministry. The importance of the intellectual preparation of the student for the ministry is the reason of the existence of our Theological Seminaries. Say what you will, do what you will, the ministry is a 'learned profession'; and the man without learning, no matter with what other gifts he may be endowed, is unfit for its duties. But learning, though indispensable, is not the most indispensable thing for a minister. 'Apt to teach' – yes, the minister must be 'apt to teach'; and observe that what I say – or rather what Paul says – is 'apt to *teach*'. Not apt merely to exhort, to beseech, to appeal, to entreat; not even merely to testify, to bear witness; but to *teach*. And teaching implies knowledge: he who teaches must know. Paul, in other words, requires of you, as we are perhaps learning not very felicitously to phrase it, 'instructional', not merely 'inspirational', service. But aptness to teach alone does not make a minister; nor is it his primary qualification. It is only one of a long list of requirements which Paul lays down as necessary to meet in him who aspires to this high office. And all the rest concern, not his intellectual, but his spiritual fitness. A minister must be learned, on pain of being utterly incompetent for his work. But before and above being learned, a minister must be godly.

Nothing could be more fatal, however, than to set these two things over against one another. Recruiting officers do not dispute whether it is better for soldiers to have a right leg or a left leg: soldiers should have both legs. Sometimes we hear it said that ten minutes on your knees will give you a truer, deeper, more operative knowledge of God than ten hours over your books. 'What!' is the appropriate response, 'than ten hours over your books, on your knees?' Why should you turn from God when you turn to your books, or feel that you must turn from your books in order to turn to God? If learning and devotion are as antagonistic as that, then the intellectual life is in itself accursed, and there can be no question of a religious life for a student, even of theology. The mere fact that he is a student inhibits religion for him. That I am asked to speak to you on the religious life of the student of theology proceeds on the recognition of the absurdity of such antitheses. You are students of theology; and, just because you are students of theology, it is understood that you are religious men – especially religious men, to whom the cultivation of your religious life is a matter of the profoundest concern – of such concern that you will wish above all things to be warned of the dangers that may assail your religious life, and be pointed to the means by which you may strengthen and enlarge it. In your case there can be no 'either/or' here – 'either' a student 'or' a man of God. You must be both.

Perhaps the intimacy of the relation between the work of a theological student and his religious life will nevertheless bear some emphasizing. Of course you do not think religion and study incompatible. But it is barely possible that there may be some among you who think of them too much apart – who are inclined to set their studies off to one side, and their religious life off to the other side, and to fancy that what is given to the one is taken from the other. No mistake could be more gross. Religion does not take a man away from his work; it sends him to his work with an added quality of devotion. We sing – do we not? –

> Teach me, my God and King,
> In all things Thee to see –
> And what I do in anything,
> To do it as for Thee.
> If done t' obey Thy laws,
> E'en servile labours shine,
> Hallowed is toil, if this the cause,
> The meanest work divine.

It is not just the way George Herbert wrote it. He put, perhaps, a sharper point on it. He reminds us that a man may look at his work as he looks at a pane of glass – either seeing nothing but the glass, or looking straight through the glass to the wide heavens beyond. And he tells us plainly that there is nothing so mean but that the great words, 'for thy sake', can glorify it:

A servant, with this clause,
Makes drudgery divine,
Who sweeps a room as for Thy laws,
Makes that, and the action, fine.

But the doctrine is the same, and it is the doctrine, the fundamental doctrine, of Protestant morality, from which the whole system of Christian ethics unfolds. It is the great doctrine of 'vocation', the doctrine, to wit, that the best service we can offer to God is just to do our duty – our plain, homely duty, whatever that may chance to be. The Middle Ages did not think so; they cut a cleft between the religious and the secular life, and counselled him who wished to be religious to turn his back on what they called 'the world', that is to say, not the wickedness that is in the world – 'the world, the flesh and the devil', as we say – but the work-a-day world, that congeries [*i.e. mass*] of occupations which forms the daily task of men and women, who perform their duty to themselves and their fellowmen. Protestantism put an end to all that. As Professor Doumergue eloquently puts it:

> Then Luther came, and, with still more consistency, Calvin, proclaiming the great idea of 'vocation', an idea and a word which are found in the languages of all the Protestant peoples – *Beruf, Calling, Vocation* – and which are lacking in the languages of the peoples of antiquity and of medieval culture. 'Vocation' – it is the call of God, addressed to every man, whoever he may be, to lay upon him a particular work, no matter what. And the calls, and therefore also the called, stand on a complete equality with one another. The burgomaster is God's burgomaster; the physician is God's physician; the merchant is God's merchant; the labourer is God's labourer. Every vocation, liberal, as we call it, or manual, the humblest and the vilest in appearance as truly as the noblest and the most glorious, is of divine right.

Talk of the divine right of kings! Here is the divine right of every workman, no one of whom needs to be ashamed, if only he is an honest and good workman. 'Only laziness,' adds Professor Doumergue, 'is ignoble, and while Romanism multiplies its mendicant orders, the Reformation banishes the idle from its towns.'

Now, as students of theology your vocation is to study theology; and to study it diligently, in accordance with the apostolic injunction: 'Whatsoever ye do, do it heartily, as to the Lord' [Col. 3:23 KJV]. It is precisely for this that you are students of theology; this is your 'next duty', and the neglect of duty is not a fruitful religious exercise. Dr Charles Hodge, in his delightful autobiographical notes, tells of Philip Lindsay, the most popular professor in the Princeton College of his day – a man sought by nearly every college in the Central States for its presidency – that 'he told our class that we would find that one of the best preparations for death was a thorough knowledge of the Greek grammar'. 'This,' comments Dr Hodge, in his quaint fashion, 'was his way of telling us that we ought to do our duty.' Certainly, every man who aspires to be a religious man must begin by doing his duty, his obvious duty, his daily task, the particular work which lies before him to do at this particular time and place. If this work happens to be studying, then his religious life depends on nothing more fundamentally than on just studying. You might as well talk of a father who neglects his parental duties, of a son who fails in all the obligations of filial piety, of an artisan who systematically skimps his work and turns in a bad job, of a workman who is nothing better than an eye-servant, being religious men as of a student who does not study being a religious man. It cannot be: you cannot build up a religious life except you begin by performing faithfully your simple, daily duties. It is not the question whether you like these duties. You may think of your studies what you please. You may consider that you are singing precisely of them when you sing of 'e'en servile labours', and of 'the meanest work'. But you must faithfully give yourselves to your studies, if you wish to be religious men. No religious character can be built up on the foundation of neglected duty.

There is certainly something wrong with the religious life of a theological student who does not study. But it does not quite follow that therefore everything is right with his religious life if he does study. It is possible to study – even to study theology – in an entirely secular spirit. I said a little while ago that what religion does is to send a man to his work with an added quality of devotion. In saying that, I meant the word 'devotion' to be taken in both its senses – in the sense of 'zealous application', and in the sense of 'a religious exercise', as the Standard Dictionary phrases the two definitions. A truly religious man will study anything which it becomes his duty to study with 'devotion' in both of these senses. That is what his religion does for him: it makes him do his duty, do it thoroughly, do it 'in the Lord'. But in the case of many branches of study, there is nothing in the topics studied which tends directly to feed the religious life, or to set in movement the religious emotions, or to call out specifically religious reaction. If we study them 'in the Lord,' that is only because we do it 'for his sake', on the principle which makes 'sweeping a room' an act of worship. With theology it is not so. In all its branches alike, theology has as its unique end to make God known: the student of theology is brought by his daily task into the presence of God, and is kept there. Can a religious man stand in the presence of God, and not worship? It is possible, I have said, to study even theology in a purely secular spirit. But surely that is possible only for an irreligious man, or at least for an unreligious man. And here I place in your hands at once a touchstone by which you may discern your religious state, and an instrument for the quickening of your religious life. Do you prosecute your daily tasks as students of theology as 'religious exercises'? If you do not, look to yourselves: it is surely not all right with the spiritual condition of that man who can busy himself daily with divine things, with a cold and impassive heart. If you do, rejoice. But in any case, see that you do! And that you do it ever more and more abundantly. Whatever you may have done in the past, for the future make all your theological studies 'religious exercises'. This is the great rule for a rich and wholesome religious life in a theological student. Put your heart into your studies; do not merely occupy your mind with them, but put your heart into them. They bring you daily and hourly into the very presence of God; his ways, his dealing with men, the infinite majesty of his Being form their very subject-matter. Put the shoes from off your feet in this holy presence!

We are frequently told, indeed, that the great danger of the theological student lies precisely in his constant contact with divine things. They may come to seem common to him, because they are customary. As the average man breathes the air and basks in the sunshine without ever a thought that it is God in his goodness who makes his sun to rise on him, though he is evil, and sends rain to him, though he is unjust; so you may come to handle even the furniture of the sanctuary with never a thought above the gross earthly materials of which it is made. The words which tell you of God's terrible majesty or of his glorious goodness may come to be mere words to you – Hebrew and Greek words, with etymologies, and inflections, and connections in sentences. The reasonings which establish to you the mysteries of his saving activities may come to be to you mere logical paradigms, with premises and conclusions, fitly framed, no doubt, and triumphantly cogent, but with no further significance to you than their formal logical conclusiveness. God's stately steppings in his redemptive processes may become to you a mere series of facts of history, curiously interplaying to the production of social and religious conditions, and pointing mayhap to an issue which we may shrewdly conjecture: but much like other facts occurring in time and space, which may come to your notice. It *is* your great danger. But it is your great danger only because it is your great privilege. Think of what your privilege is when your greatest danger is that the great things of religion may become common to you! Other men, oppressed by the hard conditions of life, sunk in the daily struggle for bread perhaps, distracted at any rate by the dreadful drag of the world upon them and the awful rush of the world's work, find it hard to get time and opportunity so much as to pause and consider whether there be such things as God, and religion, and salvation from the sin that compasses them about and holds them captive. The very atmosphere of your life is these things; you breathe them in at every pore; they surround you, encompass you, press in upon you from every side. It is all in danger of becoming common to you! God forgive you, you are in danger of becoming weary of God!

Do you know what this danger is? Or, rather, let us turn the question – are you alive to what your privileges are? Are you making full use of them? Are you, by this constant contact with divine things, growing in holiness, becoming every day more and more men of God?

If not, you are hardening! And I am here today to warn you to take seriously your theological study, not merely as a duty, done for God's sake and therefore made divine, but as a religious exercise, itself charged with religious blessing to you; as fitted by its very nature to fill all your mind and heart and soul and life with divine thoughts and feelings and aspirations and achievements. You will never prosper in your religious life in the Theological Seminary until your work in the Theological Seminary becomes itself to you a religious exercise out of which you draw every day enlargement of heart, elevation of spirit and adoring delight in your Maker and your Saviour.

I am not counselling you, you will observe, to make your theological studies your sole religious exercises. They are religious exercises of the most rewarding kind; and your religious life will very much depend upon your treating them as such. But there are other religious exercises demanding your punctual attention which cannot be neglected without the gravest damage to your religious life. I refer particularly now to the stated formal religious meetings of the Seminary. I wish to be perfectly explicit here, and very emphatic. No man can withdraw himself from the stated religious services of the community of which he is a member, without serious injury to his personal religious life. It is not without significance that the apostolic writer couples together the exhortations, 'to hold fast the confession of our hope, that it waver not' [Heb. 10:23 ASV], and 'to forsake not the assembling of ourselves together' [Heb. 10:25 KJV]. When he commands us not to forsake 'the assembling of ourselves together', he has in mind, as the term he employs shows, the stated, formal assemblages of the community, and means to lay upon the hearts and consciences of his readers their duty to the church of which they are the supports, as well as their duty to themselves. And when he adds, 'As the custom of some is', he means to put a lash into his command. We can see his lip curl as he says it. Who are these people, who are so vastly strong, so supremely holy, that they do not need the assistance of the common worship for themselves; and who, being so strong and holy, will not give their assistance to the common worship?

Needful as common worship is, however, for men at large, the need of it for men at large is as nothing compared with its needfulness for a body of young men situated as you are. You are gathered together here for a religious purpose, in preparation for the highest religious service which can be performed by men – the guidance of others in the religious life; and shall you have everything else in common except worship? You are gathered together here, separated from your homes and all that home means; from the churches in which you have been brought up, and all that church fellowship means; from all the powerful natural influences of social religion – and shall you not yourselves form a religious community, with its own organic religious life and religious expression? I say it deliberately, that a body of young men, living apart in a community-life, as you are and must be living, cannot maintain a healthy, full, rich religious life individually, unless they are giving organic expression to their religious life as a community in frequent stated diets of common worship. Nothing can take the place of this common organic worship of the community as a community, at its stated seasons, and as a regular function of the corporate life of the community. Without it you cease to be a religious community and lack that support and stay, that incitement and spur, that comes to the individual from the organic life of the community of which he forms a part.

In my own mind, I am quite clear that in an institution like this the whole body of students should come together, both morning and evening, every day, for common prayer; and should join twice on every Sabbath in formal worship. Without at least this much common worship I do not think the institution can preserve its character as a distinctively religious institution – an institution whose institutional life is primarily a religious one. And I do not think that the individual students gathered here can, with less full expression of the organic religious life of the institution, preserve the high level of religious life on which, as students of theology they ought to live. You will observe that I am not merely exhorting you 'to go to church'. 'Going to church' is in any case good. But what I am exhorting you to do is go to your own church – to give your presence and active religious participation to every stated meeting for worship of the institution as an institution. Thus you will do your part to give to the institution an organic religious life, and you will draw out from the organic religious life of the institution a support and inspiration for your own personal religious life which you can get nowhere else, and which you cannot afford to miss – if, that is, you have a care to your religious quickening and growth. To be an active member of a living religious body is the condition of healthy religious functioning.

I trust you will not tell me that the stated religious exercises of the Seminary are too numerous, or are wearying. That would only be to betray the low ebb of your own religious vitality. The feet of him whose heart is warm with religious feeling turn of themselves to the sanctuary, and carry him with joyful steps to the house of prayer. I am told that there are some students who do not find themselves in a prayerful mood in the early hours of a winter morning; and are much too tired at the close of a hard day's work to pray, and therefore do not find it profitable to attend prayers in the late afternoon: who think the preaching at the regular service on Sabbath morning dull and uninteresting, and who do not find Christ at the Sabbath afternoon conference. Such things I seem to have heard before; and yours will be an exceptional pastorate if you do not hear something very like them before you have been in a pastorate six months. Such things meet you every day on the street; they are the ordinary expression of the heart which is dulled or is dulling to the religious appeal. They are not hopeful symptoms among those whose life should be lived on the religious heights. No doubt, those who minister to you in spiritual things should take them to heart. And you who are ministered to must take them to heart, too. And let me tell you straight-out that the preaching you find dull will no more seem dull to you if you faithfully obey the Master's precept: 'Take heed what ye hear' [Mark 4:24 KJV]; that if you do not find Christ in the conference room it is because you do not take him there with you; that, if after an ordinary day's work you are too weary to unite with your fellows in closing the day with common prayer, it is because the impulse to prayer is weak in your heart. If there is no fire in the pulpit it falls to you to kindle it in the pews. No man can fail to meet with God in the sanctuary if he takes God there with him.

How easy it is to roll the blame of our cold hearts over upon the shoulders of our religious leaders! It is refreshing to observe how Luther, with his breezy good sense, dealt with complaints of lack of attractiveness in his evangelical preachers. He had not sent them out to please people, he said, and their function was not to interest or to entertain; their function was to teach the saving truth of God, and, if they did that, it was frivolous for people in danger of perishing for want of the truth to object to the vessel in which it was offered to them.

When the people of Torgau, for instance, wished to dismiss their pastors, because, they said, their voices were too weak to fill the churches, Luther simply responded, 'That's an old song: better have some difficulty in hearing the gospel than no difficulty at all in hearing what is very far from the gospel.' 'People cannot have their ministers exactly as they wish,' he declares again. 'They should thank God for the pure word,' and not demand St Augustines and St Ambroses to preach it to them. If a pastor pleases the Lord Jesus and is faithful to him – there is none so great and mighty – but he ought to be pleased with him, too. The point, you see, is that men who are hungry for the truth and get it ought not to be exigent [*i.e. demanding*] as to the platter in which it is served to them. And they will not be.

But why should we appeal to Luther? Have we not the example of our Lord Jesus Christ? Are we better than he? Surely, if ever there was one who might justly plead that the common worship of the community had nothing to offer him it was the Lord Jesus Christ. But every Sabbath found him seated in his place among the worshipping people, and there was no act of stated worship which he felt himself entitled to discard. Even in his most exalted moods, and after his most elevating experiences, he quietly took his place with the rest of God's people, sharing with them in the common worship of the community. Returning from that great baptismal scene, when the heavens themselves were rent to bear him witness that he was well pleasing to God; from the searching trials of the wilderness, and from that first great tour in Galilee, prosecuted, as we are expressly told, 'in the power of the Spirit'; he came back, as the record tells, 'to Nazareth, where he had been brought up, and' – so proceeds the amazing narrative – 'he entered, as his custom was, into the synagogue, on the Sabbath day' [Luke 4:14-16 ASV]. 'As his custom was!' Jesus Christ made it his habitual practice to be found in his place on the Sabbath day at the stated place of worship to which he belonged. 'It is a reminder,' as Sir William Robertson Nicoll well insists, 'of the truth which, in our fancied spirituality, we are apt to forget – '

> that the holiest personal life can scarcely afford to dispense with stated forms of devotion, and that the regular public worship of the church, for all its local imperfections and dullness, is a divine provision for sustaining the individual soul.
>
> We cannot afford to be wiser than our Lord in this matter. If anyone could have pled that his spiritual experience was so lofty that it did not require public worship, if any one might have felt that the consecration and communion of his personal life exempted him from what ordinary mortals needed, it was Jesus. But he made no such plea. Sabbath by Sabbath even he was found in the place of worship, side by side with God's people, not for the mere sake of setting a good example, but for deeper reasons. Is it reasonable, then, that any of us should think we can safely afford to dispense with the pious custom of regular participation with the common worship of our locality?

Is it necessary for me to exhort those who would fain [*i.e. eagerly*] be like Christ, to see to it that they are imitators of him in this?

But not even with the most assiduous use of the corporate expressions of the religious life of the community have you reached the foundation-stone of your piety. That is to be found, of course, in your closets, or rather in your hearts, in your private religious exercises, and in your intimate religious aspirations. You are here as theological students;

and if you would be religious men, you must do your duty as theological students; you must find daily nourishment for your religious life in your theological studies: you must enter fully into the organic religious life of the community of which you form a part. But to do all this you must keep the fires of religious life burning brightly in your heart; in the inmost core of your being, you must be men of God. Time would fail me, if I undertook to outline with any fullness the method of the devout life. Every soul seeking God honestly and earnestly finds him, and, in finding him, finds the way to him. One hint I may give you, particularly adapted to you as students for the ministry: Keep always before your mind the greatness of your calling, that is to say, these two things: the immensity of the task before you and the infinitude of the resources at your disposal. I think it has not been idly said, that if we face the tremendous difficulty of the work before us, it will certainly throw us back upon our knees; and if we worthily gauge the power of the gospel committed to us, that will certainly keep us on our knees. I am led to single out this particular consideration, because it seems to me that we have fallen upon an age in which we very greatly need to recall ourselves to the seriousness of life and its issues, and to the seriousness of our calling as ministers to life. Sir Oliver Lodge informs us that 'men of culture are not bothering', nowadays, 'about their sin, much less about their punishment', and Dr Johnston Ross preaches us a much-needed homily from that text on the 'light-heartedness of the modern religious quest'. In a time like this, it is perhaps not strange that careful observers of the life of our Theological Seminaries tell us that the most noticeable thing about it is a certain falling off from the intense seriousness of outlook by which students of theology were formerly characterised.

Let us hope it is not true. If it were true, it would be a great evil; so far as it is true, it is a great evil. I would call you back to this seriousness of outlook, and bid you cultivate it, if you would be men of God now, and ministers who need not be ashamed hereafter. Think of the greatness of the minister's calling; the greatness of the issues which hang on your worthiness or your unworthiness for its high functions; and determine once for all that with God's help you will be worthy. 'God had but one Son,' says Thomas Goodwin, 'and he made him a minister.' 'None but he who made the world,' says John Newton, 'can make a minister' – that is, a minister who is worthy.

You can, of course, be a minister of a sort, and not be God-made. You can go through the motions of the work, and I shall not say that your work will be in vain – for God is good and who knows by what instruments he may work his will of good for men? Helen Jackson pictures far too common an experience when she paints the despair of one whose sowing, though not unfruitful for others, bears no harvest in his own soul.

> O teacher, then I said, thy years,
> Are they not joy? each word that issueth
> From out thy lips, doth it return to bless
> Thine own heart manyfold?

Listen to the response:

> I starve with hunger treading out their corn,
> I die of travail while their souls are born.

She does not mean it in quite the evil part in which I am reading it. But what does Paul mean when he utters that terrible warning: 'Lest when I have preached to others, I myself should be a castaway'? [1 Cor. 9:27 KJV]. And there is an even more dreadful contingency. It is our Saviour himself who tells us that it is possible to compass sea and land to make one proselyte, and when we have made him to make him twofold more a child of hell than we are ourselves. [Matt. 23:15] And will we not be in awful peril of making our proselytes children of hell if we are not ourselves children of heaven? Even physical waters will not rise above their source: the spiritual floods are even less tractable to our commands. There is no mistake more terrible than to suppose that activity in Christian work can take the place of depth of Christian affections.

This is the reason why many good men are shaking their heads a little today over a tendency which they fancy they see increasing among our younger Christian workers to restless activity at the apparent expense of depth of spiritual culture. Activity, of course, is good: surely in the cause of the Lord we should run and not be weary.

But not when it is substituted for inner religious strength. We cannot get along without our Marthas. But what shall we do when, through all the length and breadth of the land, we shall search in vain for a Mary? Of course the Marys will be as little admired by the Marthas today as of yore. 'Lord,' cried Martha, 'dost thou not care that my sister hath left me to serve alone?' [Luke 10:40 KJV]. And from that time to this the cry has continually gone up against the Marys that they waste the precious ointment which might have been given to the poor, when they pour it out to God, and are idle when they sit at the Master's feet.

A minister, high in the esteem of the churches, is even quoted as declaring – not confessing, mind you, but publishing abroad as something in which he gloried – that he has long since ceased to pray: he *works*. 'Work and pray' is no longer, it seems, to be the motto of at least ministerial life. It is to be all work and no praying; the only prayer that is prevailing, we are told, with the same cynicism with which we are told that God is on the side of the largest battalions, is just work. You will say this is an extreme case. Thank God, it is. But in the tendencies of our modern life, which all make for ceaseless – I had almost said thoughtless, meaningless – activity, have a care that it does not become your case; or that your case – even now – may not have at least some resemblance to it. Do you pray? How much do you pray? How much do you love to pray? What place in your life does the 'still hour', alone with God, take?

I am sure that if you once get a true glimpse of what is the ministry of the cross, for which you are preparing, and of what you, as men preparing for this ministry, should be, you will pray: 'Lord, who is sufficient for these things?'[2 Cor. 3:16 KJV]. Your heart will cry; and your whole soul will be wrung with the petition: Lord, make me sufficient for these things. Old Cotton Mather wrote a great little book once, to serve as a guide to students for the ministry. The not very happy title which he gave it is *Manductio ad Ministerium* ('Directions for a candidate of the ministry'). But by a stroke of genius he added a subtitle which is more significant. And this is the subtitle he added: *The angels preparing to sound the trumpets*. That is what Cotton Mather calls you, students for the ministry: the angels, preparing to sound the trumpets! Take the name to yourselves, and live up to it. Give your days and nights to living up to it! And then, perhaps, when you come to sound the trumpets the note will be pure and clear and strong, and perchance may pierce even to the grave and wake the dead.

5

Becoming Real Theologians

Dietrich Bonhoeffer

Dietrich Bonhoeffer (1906–1945) was the German pastor and theologian whose promising early work in theology was cut short by Nazi execution a month before the end of World War II. Readers have long enjoyed his sensitive and almost poetic insights. His legacy has not been without controversy, with everyone from conservatives to liberals appropriating his ideas.

Born to a well-educated secular family, his choice of a theological career disappointed his parents. He moved away from the nineteenth-century liberal tradition of his early training, recognising the necessity for divine revelation to make sense of our lived experience.

The following advice from Bonhoeffer[1] begins straightforwardly enough. But we soon become aware of the overshadowing rise of Nazism, when Bonhoeffer took his place among the minority 'Confessing Church' and opposed the apostate 'German Christians'. This compromised church willingly accepted the Nazi mythology of a special German destiny with Hitler as the Church's 'leader'. It baptised Nazi ideology in Christian language. Hence Bonhoeffer slyly refers to the way 'new, strange content hides behind the old words', which real theologians 'see with their educated eye'.

---

1. Dietrich Bonhoeffer, 'Was soll der Student der Theologie heute tun?', in *Gesammelte Schriften III* (1933), pp. 243-324; tr. Kay Avery and Brian Rosner.

He highlights the theologian's temptation simply to endorse prevailing local cultures. In dangerous times, when theology and culture have become sinisterly confused, theologians are called to speak the gospel's truth with utter clarity, and over and above the tactics of immediate political considerations – while never forgetting that they 'stand alongside their mistaken and misled brothers and sisters, sharing their guilt', relying on Christ's forgiveness and speaking with love. Bonhoeffer's magnificent confidence in the gospel – even against Nazism – reminds us of what students, pastors and theologians really have to work with.

A person should in the first place only study theology if they sincerely desire to do so and simply cannot bring themselves to study something else. It is much less of a pity when many people, who perhaps could have become good theologians, instead become good lawyers or doctors, than when a single person becomes a theologian, who really should not have done so. A large number of theologians in the younger generation is always an ambiguous phenomenon.

However, the person who actually thinks that he or she is only able to study theology should not imagine that they are better in any way than other students. They will learn by experience that the reasons which drove them to study theology will gradually fall away during their studies, so that at the end of genuine study they must be a theologian for quite different reasons – if they still must be one.

Students of theology should also not imagine that they have to wait for some definite experience of a 'vocational call'. Rather, their call to study theology consists of the fact that the subject has simply enthralled them and refuses to let them go. Of course, it must really be theology that has captivated them. There must be a genuine readiness to meditate on God, his word and his will; 'their delight is in the law of the Lord day and night' [Ps. 1:2]. They must be prepared to work intensely, to learn well and to think hard. It is not a vocational experience that stands at the threshold of theological study, but a readiness to undertake sober, serious, conscientious work.

The student may bring to their theological studies their own philosophical, ethical, educational, national and social passions. Such things make them whole persons, and as theologians they must indeed be whole persons. But as theologians they must learn that their life and thought cannot derive its momentum from any source other than the Passion of Jesus Christ, our crucified Lord. The study of theology cannot be pursued with the unrestrained energy of human passions. The true study of sacred theology begins when a person takes their searching and questions right up to the cross. In the suffering of God amidst the hatred of men they will recognise the end of all their passions and become aware of the condemnation of all their strivings. A great reversal occurs at the cross, which represents a turning-point for the study of theology. The work of theology consists not of the individual's passions, nor of a monologue or even a religious self-actualisation, but instead it consists of responsible hearing and learning, of paying attention to the word of God in the midst of a hostile world. In view of the profound importance of its subject matter, theological study is undertaken through a lessening of oneself.

A young theologian should openly and honestly seek to be a theologian in this sense, or he or she should give up theological studies as soon as possible. Young theologians should not be ashamed of their study of theology nor try to minimise it in various ways. How is it appropriate to speak disparagingly about theology, as some have from their first semester right up to their appointment to the highest offices of the church? How could it be a good thing to ignore the insights of sincere theologians such as Paul, Augustine, Thomas and those leading up to Luther? How could their questions and answers, which have for centuries mattered so much to serious-minded students, be dismissed so scornfully? Such conceit is simply badly disguised ignorance. How will such a person cope when the question arises unexpectedly, 'Am I in the right place? Should I be doing something else, something more enticing, visible and impressive?' Is someone really qualified to be a theologian if they play to the crowd by feigning indifference to theology? Since when does it befit a Christian to speak arrogantly about things they secretly do not understand?

Young theologians should understand that they study theology in the service of the true church of Christ, which acknowledges its Lord unflinchingly, and they must embrace this responsibility. It is a repugnant sight when a theologian, once graduated, neglects this, when he feels it somehow more comforting to be considered a man of the world than a theologian. Instead of winning the other person through such behaviour, they only provoke scorn that is limitless and justified. In this way they expose both themselves and theology once again to the well-founded laughter of the world. The theologian who always wants to be an exception, who likes to listen when he or she is praised at the expense of their colleagues, in the long run achieves only the opposite. Moreover, worldliness, which puts on airs and graces, actually plays nasty tricks on those who fall prey to it. It really is incomprehensible why worldliness should be considered the decisive criterion for a good theologian.

Young theologians should use their study as preparation for the task of testing the spirits in the church of Christ. They should learn from the Holy Scriptures and the confessions of the Reformation what constitutes the pure and true teaching of the gospel of Christ and be able to discern what human teaching, human law, false teaching and idolatry is. They should learn during their study not to turn black into white, but to call truth, truth, and heresy, heresy. They should consider and declare such things, carefully, modestly and objectively but also quite resolutely and boldly. Anyone who doesn't do that will answer for it themselves before the Lord of the church whom they serve! They should learn where the source of life for the church lies and how it can become obstructed and poisoned. They must learn to recognise where and when the church of Christ stands in the hour of crisis, of 'having to confess', *im status confessionis*.

And if the church they serve is in 'the state of confession' (*status confessionis*), they must acknowledge that the gospel is being turned into heresy. They must see with their educated eye that new, strange content hides behind the old words. Then, wherever they are, they will have to speak out boldly. Nothing is more important for the student of theology than to inquire more and more carefully, more and more objectively, more and more openly, more and more in love, concerning the truth of the gospel.

At such times the student should not think and act emotionally but should do so rationally and soberly. He or she shouldn't just want to play out a role, but should read and study the Bible as never before.

At such times the student should know that under no circumstances can he or she serve the church with some kind of tactical reflections, but only with the unvarnished truth.

Even the best thought-out political solutions only serve to act as a smokescreen. The student's duty is to continue to do theology in a pure and objective way.

At such times the student should be cautious rather than brash. For the pretence of confident and impetuous speech has nothing to do with the certainty of repentance and the gospel.

Finally, as true theologians they should know that even where their grasp of the truth and purity of the gospel of Jesus Christ sets them apart from heresy they nonetheless stand alongside their mistaken and misled brothers and sisters, sharing their guilt and interceding on their behalf. True theologians don't rely on know-it-all dogmatism, but solely on the forgiveness of sins.

In such times of confusion, the theologian must once more begin again, by going back to the sources, to the actual Bible and to Luther himself. The theologian must always remain cheerful and undaunted, 'speaking the truth in love' [Eph. 4:15].

6

Inner Circles and True Inclusion

C.S. Lewis

Clive Staples Lewis (1898–1963) was a highly regarded teacher of English literature at Oxford University from 1925 to 1954. During much of this period he travelled and spoke widely about what convinced him to become and remain a Christian. But it seems likely that this 'hobby' caused him to be sidelined from academic advancement while at Oxford.

This experience of exclusion seems to have taught him a lot about our longing to 'belong'. In appreciation of his writing on this theme, Andrew Cameron *extends Lewis's thought to the theological context. Lewis's diagnosis of the human drive to belong, and of how it may destroy us, is as directly relevant to those who study theology as to any other human group.*

Most of the contributions in this book pay special attention to some of the specific difficulties associated with theological learning. This chapter takes a different path. I want to observe a major occupational hazard for students of theology and for people in Christian ministry. It is not a hazard unique to those tasks, yet it does seem to beset us very much.

It is a hazard that stems from a typical human failing experienced by everyone. But it requires our special attention, because to fail in this way is utterly to deny a central element of the Christian gospel, leaving our preaching, teaching and pastoring hollow and self-contradictory. Yet unlike our more obvious sins (such as greed, laziness or sexual immorality), this failure blends too easily into the many human interactions of Christian activity and can sit unnoticed for years.

I refer to our passion to belong to some 'inner circle' of people who hover temptingly beyond our reach. When gripped by this passion, to be excluded from these circles drives us slightly mad, and to enter them leaves us smugly exultant. This very personal and subjective experience can drive dozens of our daily decisions. C.S. Lewis has called it 'the quest for the Inner Ring'.[1]

Lewis did not think of himself as a theologian, and his early thoughts about this 'quest' were not directed to theological students. Yet this problem is obviously very pressing in the lives of the theological students and ministers, but remains largely unexplored by those theologians who offer advice to students. I will therefore take the liberty of devoting some space to the problem, with C.S. Lewis as our guide. I will expand upon his thought to show its applicability to the lives of theological students and Christian ministers, and will then gesture towards some of the ways that according to the Bible, God releases us from this heartbreaking obsession.[2]

---

1. For a more detailed account of Lewis's thought about 'The Inner Ring', see Andrew Cameron, 'The "Great Permanent Mainspring": C.S. Lewis on The Inner Ring', (2006); online: http://www.cslewistoday.com/conference-2006/the-great-permanent-mainspring-cs-lewis-on-the-inner-ring (accessed 12th October, 2009).

2. The longing for entry into the 'Inner Ring' is an example of obsession; but there are many versions of obsession. For a more general investigation of the way our desires turn into obsessions and of how theology can help us, see Andrew Cameron, 'Augustine on Obsession', in *The Consolations of Theology*, ed. Brian S. Rosner (Grand Rapids: Eerdmans, 2008).

In his work of science-fiction called *That Hideous Strength*, Lewis introduces Mark Studdock, a young man who has recently begun working at 'Bracton College'. He feels like an outsider there, and longs to be accepted by 'Curry's gang'. Then, unexpectedly, Curry takes Studdock into his confidence:

> You would never have guessed from the tone of Studdock's reply what intense pleasure he derived from Curry's use of the pronoun 'we'. So very recently he had been an outsider, watching the proceedings of what he then called 'Curry and his gang' with awe and with little understanding ... Now he was inside and 'Curry and his gang' had become 'we' or 'the Progressive Element in College'. It had all happened quite suddenly and was still sweet in the mouth.
>
> ... He did not like things which reminded him that he had once been not only outside the Progressive Element but even outside the College. He did not always like Curry either. His pleasure in being with him was not that sort of pleasure.[3]

The thoughts and feelings that Studdock experiences here are what Lewis called 'one of the great permanent mainsprings of human action'. Studdock, an earnest and insecure young man, becomes involved in a plot by the National Institute for Controlled Experiments (NICE) to deliver Britain over to fascism. The NICE agenda includes indoctrination, eugenics, sterilisation and ethnic cleansing.[4] Bit by bit, Studdock's involvement erodes him.

---

3. C.S. Lewis, 'That Hideous Strength', in *The Cosmic Trilogy* (London: Pan, 1990), pp. 359-60, 361; chapter 1.2.

4. Ibid. p. 387.

Students at a theological college might think of themselves as enjoying a far safer environment than Bracton College and NICE. In many ways, they are correct. The fourth-century theologian Augustine summarises the content and practices of Christian fellowship as 'the enjoyment of God and of one another in God',[5] and these obviously bear no relation to the fascism of NICE. Seminary students often enjoy an environment that can assist the Christian life in a way that working within a multinational corporation, a government office or a secular institution does not.

Oddly though, Lewis does not present fascism or NICE as the 'smoking gun' that destroyed Studdock's friendships, his integrity and almost his marriage. The real culprit lay within: an inner compulsion to be on the 'inside' – that need to become a member of the elusive and desirable groups that Lewis calls 'Inner Rings'. 'Of all the passions,' says Lewis, this 'passion for the Inner Ring is most skilful in making a man who is not yet a very bad man do very bad things.'[6]

Even so, the Studdock of Bracton College is a servile young man. Could it be that he is peculiarly prone to this enslavement in a way that many theology students are not? After all, seminaries and ministry training schemes often select

---

5. Or near equivalent – twice in *City of God* XIX.13 and once in XIX.17. Augustine, *The City of God Against the Pagans*, tr. R.W. Dyson, *Cambridge Texts in the History of Political Thought* edition (Cambridge: Cambridge University Press, 1998), pp. 938, 940, 947.

6. C.S. Lewis, 'The Inner Ring', in *Essay Collection*, ed. Lesley Walmsley (London: HarperCollins, 2000), p. 319. The address can also be found in C.S. Lewis, *Transposition and other Addresses* (London: Geoffrey Bles, 1949), pp. 55-64; C.S. Lewis, *Screwtape Proposes a Toast and Other Pieces* (Glasgow: Collins/Fount, 1977), pp. 28-40; and in C.S. Lewis, 'The Inner Ring,' in *The Weight of Glory*, ed. Walter Hooper (London: HarperCollins, 1949, 1976); online: http://faculty.millikin.edu/~moconner/in150/lewis2.html (accessed 13th November, 2009). Page references are to the Walmsley edition.

candidates on the basis of already proven habits of independent thought, leadership and integrity, even if it is understood that these have been formed in frail flesh by the power of the Holy Spirit. Are the Studdocks of this world more prone to enslavement by Inner-Ringism than followers of Christ, who study his word? Rather than answering this question directly, I simply propose to test whether what Lewis depicts can be recognised in theological study and church ministry settings.

Lewis describes the Inner Ring in a 1944 address to young graduates who, like Studdock, are at the start of their careers. (They were exclusively men, but the themes of the address are also very recognisable for women). He begins with a passage from Tolstoy, where a captain talks to a young lieutenant in a manner that subtly isolates and excludes a general. In this moment, the young lieutenant discovers that a formally organised group can include a smaller, invisible, informal group. 'You discover gradually, in almost indefinable ways, that it exists and that you are outside it; and then later, perhaps, that you are inside it.'[7] No one is formally admitted to this inner circle, yet a particular slang, spontaneous and informal passwords, and a certain style of conversation mark those who are 'in' and those who are not.

Yet this invisible group is not constant or clear. Some are obviously in; some are obviously out; and always some are borderline. If you returned six weeks later, you might find it all quite different even though no one has been formally admitted or expelled. Indeed, people can still think they are in after they have actually been pushed out. These people are very amusing for those who are really in, as are those who have never been allowed in yet think they are in. This is a way of 'belonging' by negation:

---

7.   Lewis, 'Ring', p. 314.

You yourself once you are in, want to make it hard for the next entrant, just as those who are already in made it hard for you. … [Y]our genuine Inner Ring exists for exclusion. There'd be no fun if there were no outsiders. The invisible line would have no meaning unless most people were on the wrong side of it. Exclusion is no accident: it is the essence.[8]

Back at Bracton College, Curry eagerly introduces Studdock to the sophisticated Feverstone. Studdock thinks Feverstone is another one of 'Curry's gang' – but then Feverstone mocks Curry once he leaves the room. It becomes clear that inner circles are like a layered onion: within the Curry-circle there beckons a Feverstone-circle, and suddenly Studdock hates Curry's old circle and longs for this new one. When Feverstone offers some buttery words about having read everything Studdock has written, 'the giddy sensation of being suddenly whirled up from one place to another … prevented him from speaking'.[9] So great is Studdock's longing to be noticed, and approved, that there is a moment of speechless ecstasy as the circle opens to receive him.

Perhaps thoughts and feelings like these are more muted in a theological college. Christians are less likely openly to exult in the exclusion of another, or wantonly to flaunt their 'belonging' in the face of another. Nevertheless, a variety of theological college scenarios do seem to provoke thoughts and feelings similar to what Lewis describes:

- I am new to a college and lonely, and feel an aching envy when I see a knot of three or four others who know each other from some other country, some home church, or some ministry training scheme.

---

8.   Ibid. pp. 319-20.
9.   Lewis, 'Hideous', p. 384.

- I finally master some theological jargon or concept and an accomplished senior student, who has previously taken little notice of me, suddenly smiles and nods in approval.

- I overhear the principal talking with a bishop that so-and-so is 'worth watching', and desperately wish it were me.

- A faculty member invites some student to a reading group or to some other project of which I am not a member, and I cannot stop thinking about it.

The cycle that often flares up around such moments – envy, aching yearning, exultation, and back to envy – is precisely what Lewis seeks to bring to our attention. Lewis thinks that this cycle of feelings can drive us in directions that will destroy us. In his address to the graduate students who are about to enter various careers and so become prey to these difficulties, he speaks of how the promise of inclusion might begin with a hint to do something slightly irregular. This hint will come 'over a drink or a cup of coffee, disguised as a triviality and sandwiched between two jokes'.[10] It will be to do something that others will not quite understand:

> ... but something, says your new friend, which 'we' – and at the word 'we' you try not to blush for mere pleasure – something 'we always do'. And you will be drawn in, if you are drawn in, not by desire for gain or ease, but simply because at that moment, when the cup was so near your lips, you cannot bear to be thrust back again into the cold outer world. It would be so terrible to see the other man's face – that genial, confidential, delightfully sophisticated face – turn suddenly cold and contemptuous, to know that you had been tried for the Inner Ring and rejected. And then, if you are drawn in, next week it will be something

---

10. Lewis, 'Ring', p. 318.

a little further from the rules, and next year something
further still, but all in the jolliest, friendliest spirit. It may
end in a crash, a scandal, and penal servitude: it may end
in millions, a peerage and giving the prizes at your old
school. But you will be a scoundrel.[11]

Again, we might at first think that no such evil schemes
will come our way in a theological college. But perhaps
they only take different forms: an implied invitation to
abandon ourselves to lacerating slander of some other group
or person; an expectation to talk and think mockingly
about someone; a quiet signal that it is permissible to do
unjust favours for theological friends; an implied demand
to give up on something we know to be true. Likewise in
subsequent church life: the promise of acceptance by some
desirable group of church members, if only we will quietly
join them in mocking a senior minister, or just ease up a little
bit on some moral or doctrinal position; or the promise of
acceptance by some career clergyman if only we will assist
his method of church-politicking, or talk roughly about the
poor (or even the rich), or adopt his sneering attitude to some
other local church. People in Christian training and ministry
are constantly being tested for inner circles.

When Hannah Arendt attended the trial of Adolf
Eichmann, she sought to discover where the heart of
evil lay. What would make a man so efficiently able to
timetable trains bearing hundreds of thousands of Jews
to their deaths? To her horror, Eichmann's reasons were
as bland as those of Studdock: he wanted to belong,
and to advance his career by impressing his friends and
superiors. She journeys into the heart of darkness to

---

11. Ibid. pp. 318-19.

discover that nothing real is there – just a corrupted preoccupation with the same social impulse that drives us all. That shocking discovery elicits her famous concluding description of 'the fearsome, word-and-thought-defying *banality of evil*'.[12]

But we eventually discover in bitterness that this yearning to belong never delivers peace. The 'onion' effect enslaves us to the perpetual cycle of envy, anxiety, exultation, disappointment and boredom:

> You are trying to peel an onion: if you succeed there will be nothing left. ... The circle cannot have from within the charm it had from outside. By the very act of admitting you it has lost its magic. Once the first novelty is worn off the members of this circle will be no more interesting than your old friends. ... You merely wanted to be 'in'. And that is a pleasure that cannot last. As soon as your new associates have been staled to you by custom, you will be looking for another Ring. The rainbow's end will still be ahead of you. The old Ring will now be only the drab background for your endeavour to enter the new one.[13]

I will risk a personal reflection from my own context, where I am an ordained person in a prominent Anglican Diocese, and a member of a well-regarded theological college faculty. Some would regard these positions as enviable. But along the way I have felt and perhaps seen in others both the yearning for the next Ring and the 'onion effect'. Invitation to a ministry training scheme; acceptance to theological college; acceptance for ordination candidature; appointment as 'senior

---

12. Hannah Arendt, *Eichmann in Jerusalem: A Report on the Banality of Evil (Revised and Enlarged)* (Harmondsworth: Penguin, 1977; originally published New York: Viking Press, 1964), p. 252.

13. Lewis, 'Ring', p. 319.

student'; landing the coveted evangelism traineeship (a kind of 'knighthood' in my tribe); ordination itself; approval by a church political party; entry to the governing Committee of our Diocese; the archdeaconry; the episcopacy ... all of these offer, in their own way, the lure of the Inner Ring. Lewis would have rebuked as folly any claim that either Australian egalitarianism or Christian culture can offer me any protection.

Oddly though, we will find Lewis defending the existence of each of these rings. I will return to that defence shortly. But for the moment we need to notice the oppressive weight of their dark side. The onion has endless layers; the sieve can never be filled; the horizon always recedes. Lewis uses these metaphors to show the endless yearning for inclusion that we carry within as we navigate such systems.

To the vast majority who have no interest in my church and its groupings, Lewis will note that there are as many forms of this longing as there are groupings of people. Invitations from the rich and famous might mean nothing to *you*; yet *you* are devoured by your desire to join a fledgling band practising in some seductive, forbidden garage. Some Saturday morning crew has not yet invited *you* to play golf with them, and your desperation and pain increases. You keep dropping in on a regular group of coffee-sippers, or card-players, or mothers and children at play, hoping for more than the usual casual and careless greeting. Your every waking moment is consumed with getting your child into that selective school across town. Or you long for some sacred space – a clubhouse, common-room or coffee shop – where there gathers that knot of people with whom you long to share 'the delicious knowledge that we, we four or five huddled here, are the people who *know*'.[14] Indeed the desire diabolically conceals itself: the company accountant (or church wheeler-dealer) pulls you aside and whispers, 'Listen mate, Albert and I saw at once that we *must* get you onto our committee.' That would be such a bore. 'It is tiring and unhealthy to lose your Saturday afternoons; but to have them free because you don't matter – that is much worse.'[15]

> My main purpose ... is simply to convince you that this desire is one of the great permanent mainsprings of human action. It is one of the factors which go to make up the world as we know it – this whole pell-mell of struggle, competition, confusion, graft, disappointment, and advertisement, and if it is one of the permanent mainsprings then you may be quite sure of this. Unless you take measures to prevent it, this desire is going to be one of the chief motives of your life, from the first day on which you enter your profession until the day when you are too old to care. That will be the natural thing – the life that will come to you of its own accord. Any other kind of life, if you lead it, will be the result of conscious and continuous effort. If you do nothing about it, if you drift with the stream, you will in fact be an 'inner ringer'. I don't say you'll be a successful one; that's as may be. But whether by pining and moping outside Rings that you can never enter, or by passing triumphantly further and further in – one way or the other you will be that kind of man. I have already made it fairly clear that I think it better for you not to be that kind of man.[16]

I urge you to read, reread and read that paragraph again, for theological students spectacularly and regularly fail in the

14. Ibid. p. 316.
15. Ibid. p. 316.
16. Lewis, 'Ring', p. 318.

way Lewis describes. One of the most dominant elements in all our lives is the desire to be inside inner circles and the terror of being left outside. Theological students and people in church ministries are no exception.

I meet a lot of people, usually Christians, who hear about 'inner rings' and make an obvious response. 'Well of course the problem is *cliques*. They are bad, aren't they?' But at this point Lewis surprises us. To expect people not to have bonds of affection, and not to gather into little knots of affinity, makes about as much sense as expecting them to give up their slavish dependence upon oxygen. Our natural interest in human social relationships is seen in God's astonishing declaration to Adam – that even when Adam was in harmonious relationship with God himself, 'it is not good for the man to be alone' [Gen. 2:18]. Although God's immediate solution is the provision of a spouse, we may also validly draw the wider inference that *humans need human company*.

There will always be a place for friendship, for shared tasks, for confidential discussions, and for circles of common interest. Inner Rings are not evil simply because they exist. Informal 'networks' simply develop while people work on projects or just 'hang around' together. 'Inner Rings' are necessary, thinks Lewis, and we should not even think of them as a necessary 'evil'. They are an unavoidable and innocent feature of life. Therefore the myriad structures of my denomination are not inherently evil. They simply represent ways in which thousands of people have banded together to follow Jesus and tell others of him. Little knots of people who like each other and work together cannot be blasted as mere 'cliques'.

We are drawn into groups by virtue, kindness, loyalty, humour, learning, wit, or common loves. 'If, say, you want to join a musical society because you really like music – then there is a possibility of satisfaction. You may find yourself playing in a quartet and you may enjoy it.'[17] Lewis's target is not the inner circles themselves, for without them, we would be left with either an undifferentiated collective or with thousands of unconnected individuals.[18] But the 'great permanent mainspring' to which he refers is a *disordering* of our proper desire for human relationship, expressed as the obsession to have it at all costs, the anguish when we are excluded, the dark side of that 'delicious sense of secret intimacy' that inclusion gives us,[19] and the pleasure of excluding others in their turn. Ever since I first read it Lewis's stark, final diagnosis has stayed with me: that 'the quest of the Inner Ring will break your hearts unless you break it'.[20] 'Until you conquer the fear of being an outsider, an outsider you will remain.'[21] The poignant humanity of this diagnosis repeats Augustine's pained recollection of himself, made 1500 years earlier: that 'there is a ... kind of temptation which, I fear, has not passed from me. Can it ever pass from me in all this life? It is the desire to be feared or loved by other men, simply for the pleasure that it gives me, though in such pleasure there is no true joy.'[22]

Lewis thinks that when we 'break' this compulsion to belong, something wonderful happens. Belonging finds us.

> [Y]ou will ... find that you have come unawares to a real inside: that you are indeed snug and safe at the centre of something which, seen from without, would look

---

17. Ibid. p. 319.

18. Cf. C.S. Lewis, 'Membership', in *The Weight of Glory*, ed. Walter Hooper (London: HarperCollins, 1949, 1976), pp. 159, 163.

19. Lewis, 'Ring', p. 317.

20. Ibid. p. 320.

21. Ibid. p. 319.

22. Augustine, *Confessions*, tr. R.S. Pine-Coffin, Penguin Classics edition (Harmondsworth: Penguin, 1961), p. 244 (X. 36).

exactly like an Inner Ring. But the difference is that its secrecy is accidental, and its exclusiveness a by-product, and no one was led thither by the lure of the esoteric: for it is only four or five people who like one another meeting to do things that they like. This is friendship. ... It causes perhaps half of all the happiness in the world, and no Inner Ring can ever have it.[23]

But *how* does Lewis think we may conquer this fear and 'break' this quest? Evangelical Christians, in lucid moments when we know ourselves most well, see only frailty and weakness – unreliable 'jars of clay' [2 Cor. 4:7]. We know that we are too easily swept up into our longings which seem so real at the time, but which prove so fruitless and empty in hindsight.

We find Lewis contemplating an odd paradox: we cannot find shelter from this storm by joining a herd, whether large or small. He knows that various large groupings are necessary, but they are transient, and are usually limited to short-term goals. He has no confidence that our longing to belong will be met by membership in some human movement or cause.[24] Even family life is inadequate finally to meet this need to belong.[25] Rather, 'the true road lies in quite another direction', and he proceeds to make cryptic mention of the Christian Scriptures.[26]

For Lewis, *all* our desires are dim anticipations of what was always *finally* intended for us by God.[27] Just as our fleeting,

---

23. Lewis, 'Ring', p. 320.

24. Lewis, 'Membership', pp. 159, 163.

25. C.S. Lewis, 'The Sermon and the Lunch', in *Undeceptions*, ed. Walter Hooper (London: Geoffrey Bles, 1971), pp. 236-7.

26. Lewis, 'Ring', p. 320.

27. 'I was sent back to the false gods there to acquire some capacity for worship against the day when the true God should recall me to himself.' C.S. Lewis,

aching moments of joy keep pointing beyond themselves to something more, so also is something similar at work in our unquenchable longings to belong. In a universe where we are constantly treated as strangers, 'we pine', 'longing to be acknowledged, to meet with some response, to bridge some chasm'.[28] Whether we realise it or not, our hunger is for 'acceptance by God, response, acknowledgement, and welcome into the heart of things'. With God, he says, 'the door on which we have been knocking all our lives will open at last',[29] and in the presence of God we find the home we have always sought. Lewis also knows the obverse truth: that from time to time we reckon with the threat of banishment from God's presence, 'left utterly and absolutely *outside* – repelled, exiled, estranged, finally and unspeakably ignored'.[30] If the longing for the Inner Ring is a harbinger of heaven, the terror of exclusion is a glimpse of hell. 'We are summoned from the outset to combine as creatures with our Creator.'[31] Lewis rediscovers what Augustine knew of human sociality: that stitched into our very marrow is the ultimate purpose of our existence – to

---

Surprised by Joy: The Shape of my Early Life (London: HarperCollins, 2002), p. 88. 'Indeed, if we consider the unblushing promises of reward and the staggering nature of the rewards promised in the Gospels, it would seem that Our Lord finds our desires not too strong, but too weak. We are half-hearted creatures, fooling about with drink and sex and ambition when infinite joy is offered us, like an ignorant child who wants to go on making mud pies in a slum because he cannot imagine what is meant by the offer of a holiday at the sea. We are far too easily pleased.' (C.S. Lewis, 'The Weight of Glory', in *The Weight of Glory*, ed. Walter Hooper [London: HarperCollins, 1949, 1976], p. 16.)

28. Lewis, 'Glory', p. 40.
29. Ibid. p. 41
30. Ibid.
31. Lewis, 'Membership', p. 166.

rest in a 'perfectly ordered and harmonious enjoyment of God and of one another in God'.[32]

The Bible is of course loaded with this way of seeing, and its entire trajectory is a stake through the heart of Inner-Ring-ism. An Almighty God has made us well. Redeeming us from sin and punishment is his ultimate way of loving us. We journey as 'exiles' toward his home. When such reality seeps into our core, our freedom from the emptiness of Inner-Ring-ism begins. Consider just three biblical examples:

First: in a series of confrontations with Ahab, the most powerful tyrant ancient Israel ever saw, the lone figure of Elijah twice declares 'As the LORD the God of Israel lives, before whom I stand ...' [1 Kings 17:1 & 18:15 NRSV]. Perhaps 'before whom I stand' is just a turn of phrase for 'whom I serve' [NIV]. But it seems to be more: despite Ahab's awful power, Elijah 'stands before', and belongs to, the massive bulk of Almighty God. Any temptation to envy the 'Inner Ring' of Ahab's court is neutralised by *this* God's 'backing'. Here is the start of what at first looks like a rugged biblical individualism – the ability not to need the crowd and its promise of false belonging. But of course 'individualism' is the wrong term: Elijah knows *true belonging* in a way that makes false belonging undesirable, boring and obsolete.

Second: the New Testament authors feel the weight of this divine backing with even greater force when they consider what Christ's death must imply. After Paul's long exploration of it in Romans 1–8, he is astounded at his conclusion:

> If God is for us, who can be against us? He who did not spare his own Son, but gave him up for us all – how will

---

32. See fn. 5 above in this chapter.

he not also, along with him, graciously give us all things? Who will bring any charge against those whom God has chosen? It is God who justifies. ... neither height nor depth, nor anything else in all creation, will be able to separate us from the love of God that is in Christ Jesus our Lord. [Rom. 8:31-33, 39]

Against *this* acceptance, the excluding sneers of an Inner Ringer can be no threat. Paul does not mean to minimise the transient pain of human condemnation and exclusion. Indeed his own frequent and sometimes awful experiences of exclusion give his statement in Romans 8 the ballast of authenticity. His point, though, is that no human condemnation can find any lasting point of attachment to the person whom God himself has forgiven and approved in Christ.

Third: in the letter to the Colossians, Paul addresses himself to a situation where esoteric 'insiders' leverage the desire for the Inner Ring, torturing vulgar 'outsiders' with tales about how as 'insiders' they adhere more strictly to food laws, more flawlessly observe religious festivals, and have seen angels. But, says Paul, 'God was pleased to have all his fullness dwell in [Christ]' [Col. 1:19]. 'All the fullness of the Deity lives in bodily form' in this Christ [Col. 2:9] – and in a brilliantly unanticipated reply to these excluders, Paul declares to the vulgar Colossian outsiders that in reality, 'you have been given fullness in Christ, who is the Head over every power and authority' [Col. 2:10]. To be with Christ in this way is to be at the centre; in fact the Colossian Inner-Ringers have 'lost connection with the Head' [Col. 2:19]. Their aloofness to Christ puts them, by their own choice, on the outside.

If I may return again to the problem of 'belonging' within the structures of my own church denomination, I am reminded of Archbishop Jensen's inaugural address to the Anglican Diocese of Sydney. There are many small churches on the geographical and social 'edge' of this large and slightly powerful institution. They often perceive themselves to be marginalised and alone. It is, in its own way, an 'inner ring' problem. But for Jensen neither the episcopacy, the denomination's structure, nor the Diocesan head office are any kind of real or final 'centre', since 'our true centre is in heaven; we march to the beat of His drum'.[33]

This view of social reality is unusual for an organisation's most senior official, and starkly counterpoints that of Studdock, Tolstoy's general, and ourselves at our most frail and driven. Christian theology shapes a powerful alternative vision of true 'belonging'. True inclusion is found, to borrow Paul's commonplace yet superb phrase, 'in Christ'.

With Lewis, I remain pessimistic about my own chances of breaking my desire for the inner circle through the 'strength' of my own will-power, or (worse) by 'believing in myself'. I may as well trust in my power never to fall ill. Rather, Lewis's comments on a related matter give some clues about how we might daily become released of our chains:

> I am not in despair. At this point I become what some would call very Evangelical; at any rate very un-Pelagian. I do not think any efforts of my own will can end once and for all this craving … Only God can. I have good faith and hope he will. Of course, I don't mean that I can therefore, as they say, 'sit back'. What God does for us, He does in us. The process of doing it will appear to me (and not falsely) to be the daily or hourly repeated exercises of my own will renouncing this attitude, especially

---

33. Peter F. Jensen, 'Presidential Address', in *Yearbook of the Diocese of Sydney* (Sydney: St Andrews House, 2002), 383 (delivered 26th October, 2001).

each morning, for it grows all over me like a new shell each night. Failures will be forgiven; it is acquiescence that is fatal ... We may never, this side of death, drive the invader out of our territory, but we must be in the Resistance, not in the Vichy government.[34] And this, so far as I can yet see, must be begun again *every day*.[35]

For theological students and workers gripped by the quest for inner circles, the 'exercises' needed are discussed throughout this book. But they are not so different than for any Christian. We remember before whom we really stand. We know the One who is 'for us'. We allow our breath to be taken away by the One who gives us his 'fullness'. We recognise the appropriateness of human loneliness, friendships, and belonging, with sadness at their absence. We enjoy friendship and belonging when, in God's kindness, they happen upon us. We prayerfully wait upon his Spirit for help in our great frailty.

---

34. Lewis is referring to the puppet French government of Nazi-occupied southern France. The metaphor is meant to highlight and oppose the way we become sold out to cultures around us.

35. C.S. Lewis, 'A Slip of the Tongue', in *The Weight of Glory*, ed. Walter Hooper (London: HarperCollins, 1949, 1976), pp. 191-2.

Part 2

VOICES PRESENT

7

The Trials of Theological College

John W. Woodhouse

Dr John W. Woodhouse has been the Principal of Moore Theological College in Sydney, Australia, since 2002. The following article is based upon his vision of life at Moore, which he regularly outlines to students in different ways and at various opportunities.

Woodhouse moves beyond the daily activities of seminary life to what we are really *there for, and how we may practise that purpose. Without this awareness, our experience of college is diminished. With it, we are enabled to see beyond the regular setbacks, irritations and shortcomings of this peculiar community. We begin to see its capacity to completely change our lives.*

Although a particular college community is on view, we believe this vision has a lot to say to anyone attending similar centres of biblical and theological study. Indirectly, it also addresses anyone charged to shape and govern any experience of theological education.

I would like to share a vision of life at theological college, because expectations are important. Your experience at college will be more profitable if you are looking for the right things. Otherwise, disappointment and frustration will be inevitable.

In sharing this vision, I will look beyond the many details of college life to the *realities* in which we are involved. These

realities are so important that if you do not see and understand them, no amenities nor buildings nor course offerings
can make up for your loss. What are we really, and why are
we here?

We are here to know God

Paul prayed for the Colossians 'that you may be filled
with the knowledge of his will in all spiritual wisdom and
understanding, so as to walk in a manner worthy of the Lord,
fully pleasing to him, bearing fruit in every good work, and
increasing in the knowledge of God' [Col. 1:9-10].[1] My longing
and desire is that each person at this college will grow in their
knowledge and love of God. I hope every student desires
that for themselves.

It follows that we will beware of pragmatism, which is
interested in mere doing, at the expense of knowing, loving
and being. It also follows that we leave here to participate in
the work that elsewhere Paul describes as God's spreading 'the
fragrance of the knowledge of him everywhere' [2 Cor. 2:14].
We prepare for that work by growing in our knowledge of
God.

The knowledge and love of God is the purpose and
intention of all that we do here, and is the measure by which
we try to assess and evaluate what we do and how we do it.
But we need to know what 'knowing God' actually means.

Knowing God is God's idea, not ours

Knowledge of God is possible for humanity not because
of some innate capacity in us, but because God wants to be
known. When Pharaoh declares 'I do not know the LORD,'
God responds that he will act so that 'they *will* know that

---

1.   Biblical quotations in this chapter are from the English Standard Version.

I am the LORD'. This important Old Testament theme finds its ultimate expression in Isaiah 11:9, where 'the earth shall be full of the knowledge of the LORD as the waters cover the sea'.

God's intention to be known has significant consequences. It is the opposite of mysticism. It also means that our ideas about God, and our ideas about what it means to know and to love God, will likely turn out to be wrong. Rather, we are here to discover God as he wills himself to be known.

Indeed, our knowledge of God requires some perspective, because it turns out that there is something more important than *our* knowledge of *God* – namely, *God's* knowledge of *us*. We could perhaps even say that *knowing God* means *knowing God knows us*:

> '… now that you have come to know God, or rather to be known by God …' [Gal. 4:9]
> '… if anyone loves God, he is known by God …' [1 Cor. 8:3]
> 'The Lord knows those who are his.' [2 Tim 2:19]

Hence knowing God is *good* because it is God's idea. This knowledge began with his knowledge of us, and is better than anything we can achieve or attain.

Knowing God is not merely a knowledge of facts

Paul speaks of a 'knowledge of the truth which accords with godliness' [Titus 1:1]. He also speaks of those who 'profess to know God, but they deny him by their works' [Titus 1:16]. He urges upon Timothy 'the teaching that accords with godliness' [1 Tim. 6:3].

Our knowledge of God is inseparably tied up with 'godliness', a theme in the Pastoral epistles that describes a certain way of living and being that goes far beyond the mere acquisition of facts. We are not here as providers and consumers in a 'fact factory', and you will be seriously mistaken about the nature of your participation if you approach it as just another intellectual or academic enterprise.

We could know the whole Bible off by heart in Greek and Hebrew; we could recite the contents of several textbooks; we could attain high distinctions in every subject – and yet, it would be perfectly possible that *we did not know God*.

Knowing God is real, not abstract; personal, not just intellectual; and will be displayed in your character and conduct, not your cleverness. That is why I think it is always helpful to link *knowing* God with *loving* God: we seek the kind of knowledge here that changes our affections.

Knowing God does involve understanding

Yet to know God includes the exercise of our understanding. For several reasons, my previous point has led in some Christian circles to various strains of anti-intellectualism. Some versions of postmodernism, mysticism or pietism try to sidestep clarity about the knowledge of God. But God wills to be known by the truth being known; and knowledge of truth is a work of the mind.

It is true that this truth has at its centre the person and work of Jesus Christ, the 'word of the cross': it is not human philosophy, or human reasoning, or human discovery. It is also true that this truth is 'foolishness to those who are perishing': it is not 'the wisdom of this age or of the rulers of this age'.

But even conceding those points, *knowing God involves using the brains God made*. It involves understanding and therefore thinking. We know God, not by a mystical experience beyond words, but by hearing the Spirit-breathed word of God. This

Spirit-breathed word of God is meant to be *understood*. It tells us the truth, and by his Spirit and through his word, God reveals to us himself, his promises and his purposes.

This is no small subject. When the Bible says, 'Oh the depth of the riches and wisdom and knowledge of God! How unsearchable are his judgments and how inscrutable his ways!' [Rom. 11:33], we are not being discouraged from searching and from seeking to understand. Rather, we are being reminded that we can never think of ourselves as having finished our exploration and our growth in understanding. What happens next is quite striking. Once we grasp just a little of the 'riches' and 'wisdom' and 'knowledge' of God, all other thinking about everything is affected.

Here is why it makes perfect sense, if the circumstances of life allow, for a person to take out one or several years of serious study to increase in the knowledge of God.

We gather as a fellowship in Christ
Various circumstances and purposes lead us to becoming involved in a theological college; and we like to think that our group has been created through sets of personal decisions made by each of us.

But we are related by something prior to all those particular factors – something more important and powerful than those incidentals. We are all 'in Christ Jesus'. When you and I meet each other, and discover that we each know Christ and are known by him, then we are not strangers. We are brothers and sisters. We are bound to each other by a spiritual bond that the Bible calls 'the unity of the Spirit' [Eph. 4:3]. 'For *through him* we both have access *in one Spirit* to the Father' [Eph. 2:18].

'Through him' refers to our Lord's death on his cross ('the blood of Christ' of Eph. 2:13 or 'the cross' of v. 16).

'Through him' refers to the agency of Jesus, by means of his death. He died for me in exactly the same way as he died for you, and for the person who sits or reads or chats next to you. Indeed, and more to the point, he died in exactly the same way and with exactly the same purpose for the person you do *not* want sitting or reading or chatting next to you.

'In one Spirit' refers to the work of the Holy Spirit of God, who has brought us into the realm opened for us by Jesus' death. The Spirit in whom you live, and who lives in you, is *one and the same Spirit* in whom I live, and who lives in me. In consequence, we each and all enjoy exactly the same access to the one Father.

Paul is at pains to bring to the minds of his Gentile readers that *this* bond exists between *all* believers, Jew and Gentile. The imperative that introduces the paragraph is 'remember' [Eph. 2:11]. The bond that joins Jew and Gentile, slave and free, male and female, also joins every other kind and variety of background and identity that is represented among us. Incredibly, before we are anything else, we are 'one in Christ Jesus' by the grace of God.

But our natural inclination will be to disbelieve this gracious gift, and our usual tendency will be to act as though we are some other kind of group. We will presume to treat one another on some other basis than oneness in Christ:

- We will presume to gather with those who look or think or speak or dress or live in some way that appeals to us. *But remember: through him we both have access in one Spirit to the Father.*

- We will presume to imagine a 'them' over against 'us', whether the 'them' is the faculty, the administration staff, our Board – or if we already belong to one of those groups, the students. *But remember: through him we both have access in one Spirit to the Father.*

- We will presume to give primacy to our institutional roles as the basis of our relationship. So I will presume mainly and only think of myself as 'Principal'; those who lead classes as 'Faculty'; and those who have been here a while as 'Third Years'; and so on. *But remember: through him we both – we all – have access in one Spirit to the Father.*

- We will presume to treat the college as a means to an education, a qualification, or a job. We will then presume that the people around us are at best an irrelevance and at worst a hindrance to those goals. *But remember: through him we all have access in one Spirit to the Father.*

The truth is extraordinary. Let us 'walk in a manner worthy of the calling to which we have been called, with all humility and gentleness, with patience, bearing with one another in love.' That is how we will 'maintain the unity of the Spirit in the bond of peace' [Eph. 4:1-3].

Will you therefore shed, before doing anything else, *any* sense of superiority you might feel towards others here? We are all here as sinners, saved only by the grace of God. Will you abandon, right now, any sense of competitiveness? Competitiveness is shabby next to the Christ on his cross.

We can only be what we are towards one another by God's grace. We therefore put a high priority on meeting together several times a week deliberately under the word of God – alongside the academic study – we take time to listen to God's word, with the specific purpose of being shaped by God's word. Our chapel and chaplaincy group meetings are a structure designed to build our fellowship in Christ. But what I want us to see here is that we *are* a fellowship in Christ. This is not something we hope to be, or wish we were, or are disappointed that we are not. Like the forgiveness of our sins, it is given by God's grace. We live and respond in the bright light of the reality God has given us.

We are partners in the gospel

The ascended Lord Jesus Christ builds his congregation, his 'church' [Matt. 16:18]. But how? In the terms of Ephesians 4, by giving 'the apostles, the prophets, the evangelists, the pastors and teachers' for 'the building up the body of Christ' [Eph. 4:11-12]. Building proceeds through the preaching and teaching of the gospel of our Lord Jesus Christ, which (to mix the metaphors) 'is bearing fruit and growing' ... 'in the whole world' [Col. 1:6].

We exist to partner in that work. In one of the greatest expressions of the paradox of divine sovereignty and human responsibility, the Lord's work of building (or 'edifying') the body of Christ also becomes what we do.

Jesus said, 'Pray earnestly to the Lord of the harvest to send out labourers into his harvest' [Matt. 9:38]. Many have been praying just that, and it seems that the Lord of the harvest is answering those prayers in your being here. So do not lose sight of the fact that what we are doing together has to do with the Lord's work of building his congregation, that 'spiritual house' made of living stones [1 Pet. 2:5], as he calls people to himself by the preaching and teaching of the gospel.

If we lose sight of that, we quickly lose direction. That would be as true of the college as a whole as of us each individually. The college might boast of the finest theological library in the land, the best theological education on offer, the most prestigious awards of their kind – but we have simply lost our way if our *partnership in the gospel* ceases to be the reason for it all.

My experience is that busyness and the pressure of particular tasks are very effective opportunities for our unbelief to surface. We see only the immediate, only the pressing, only the particular. But everything done here, from introductory Greek grammar to the mundane tasks of administration, is a partnership in the gospel. We are a department of mission.

Those who understand this pray, as Paul prayed and repeatedly urged his readers to pray, for this great work of God to build the congregation of God. They will also realise that partners in the gospel must live under the Lordship of Christ so that (again), godliness takes priority over learning. To achieve first-class honours in your course here may actually be a serious mistake. The course of study you are about to embark on is demanding and stressful. If those demands become an excuse for neglecting your marriage or your children or other responsibilities you have under the Lord, then repentance and change is what you must do. God wants godly partners in the gospel, and is not always especially impressed by distinction grades.

We are a community of scholars

But since the knowledge of God involves the use of our mind, we also gather as a community of scholars. When Paul instructed Titus to appoint elders as overseers in the towns of Crete, he said of such persons that 'he must hold firm to the trustworthy word as taught, so that he may be able to give instruction in sound doctrine and also to rebuke those who contradict it' [Titus 1:9].

Again we find a paradox. God works by his word. God's word is trustworthy. This word, which is folly to those who are perishing, is the power of God to us who are being saved [1 Cor. 1:18]. And yet this trustworthy, powerful word of God has been entrusted to us, with the responsibility to guard it, to hold firmly to it, to rightly handle it. Our partnership in the gospel demands this.

I can think of no greater human responsibility than to hold firmly to the trustworthy and faithful word of God, taught as a good deposit entrusted to us by the Holy Spirit. Only then will we be able to exhort, to comfort with sound, healthy teaching.

Our community of learning is therefore an expression of our partnership in the gospel. Our curricula, our assignments, our study programmes, our writing are correctly seen as the major activities of our College: we are a community of scholars. But these are only correct when all that work has the goal and overriding purpose of holding firm to the word of God given, that we may be able to comfort and exhort with healthy teaching – and rebuke those who contradict it.

The distortion and perversion of the word of God, the teaching of error as though it were truth, is what the human mind tends to do naturally. And what the New Testament sometimes calls 'false teaching' is not neutral. It is a disease, it destroys, and it causes harm. And mere 'scholarship' is no guarantee against it. Humble learning before God, which is faithful to the good deposit entrusted to us by the Holy Spirit [2 Tim. 1:14], is the antidote. The repeated calls in Scripture to 'remember' suggest that our spiritual memory is not good. History suggests that what is taken for granted by believers today may be forgotten by the next generation of believers, and denied by the next.

Hence our responsibility as a community of scholars is enormous. We must hold firm to the trustworthy word as taught, so that we may be able to give instruction, to comfort, to exhort with sound healthy teaching and also to rebuke those who contradict it.

We are going to beware of intellectual fads. You will encounter authors who are stimulating and challenging, who open up fresh and new ways of seeing all kinds of things. You should read them; you should understand what they are saying; you should not close your mind down. Yet your task will be to discern when stimulating writers are not holding firm to the trustworthy word – just as it is to discern when some well-known or well-liked author is failing in the same way. So we are an unusual community of scholars. There is not a lot of scholarship for its own sake here.

We are organised

So we gather to know God, as a fellowship in Christ, partnering in the gospel, as a community of godly scholars. But we are not just an amorphous mass, and I simply want to draw into proper focus what we see and experience on a daily basis. A simple way to think of our college community is in terms of the four groups that comprise it: students, faculty, support staff and supporters. One of the most delightful images of our fellowship in Christ is that of the one body with its many different members [1 Cor. 12:14-21]:

> For the body does not consist of one member but of many. If the foot should say, 'Because I am not a hand, I do not belong to the body,' that would not make it any less a part of the body. And if the ear should say, 'Because I am not an eye, I do not belong to the body,' that would not make it any less a part of the body. If the whole body were an eye, where would be the sense of hearing? If the whole body were an ear, where would be the sense of smell? But as it is, God arranged the members in the body, each one of them, as he chose. If all were a single member, where would the body be? As it is, there are many parts, yet one body. The eye cannot say to the hand, 'I have no need of you,' nor again the head to the feet, 'I have no need of you.'

It is cause for thanks to God that such a body of people has been brought together as we find here in this College. You can see this miracle all over the world, in every place where God has gathered his people – but it is no less wonderful here.

I am sure I do not need to remind you to treat with proper respect and love the members of this body who might initially appear to have a less important role among us. We have alongside us many people prepared to do many apparently mundane tasks so that the faculty is free to study and teach well, and students are free to study and learn well. Very occasionally, we speak disrespectfully to one of those who serve us. That is a denial of who we are in Christ. I know you will be careful about that.

Of course all this being said, we do not always get things right. Mistakes are made; not everything proceeds as we hope or want; we experience disagreements; and we sometimes let each other down. I know that. Our imperfections and failures will be a large part of our experience of the college.

But how we live and work together can and must be shaped by what we are, and I invite you to see what we do here through clear eyes and with true vision.

We are here to know and love God. We participate in something that began as his idea, not ours; indeed, we are here because we are known by God. Our knowledge and love of God is more than mere fact-gathering, yet it does include a proper apprehension together of the truth. We are here through Jesus, having access in one Spirit to the Father, and so we are a fellowship in Christ. As we proclaim Christ and him crucified, we are partners in the gospel. We hold firmly to the word of the cross, which constitutes the nature of our scholarship. And as we teach and study and learn, we give thanks to God for those who uphold our organisation and make possible the conditions of our study and learning.

8

The Trials of Biblical Studies

D.A. Carson

Dr Don Carson is New Testament Research Professor at Trinity Evangelical Divinity School in Deerfield, Illinois. He has taught at this institution since 1978, and his epic output in the discipline makes him well-placed to describe the dangers of 'professional' biblical study.

We begin to see how much can 'hide' beneath the noble object of our study. The magnificent and privileged collection that we call 'the Bible' is so particular in its purpose, and so special in its origin, that we call it 'Holy Scripture'. Yet its excellence distracts us from the hidden deceptions we engage in as we work on it.

Carson observes five 'domains' that students of Scripture will need to address: integration (of the Bible, and of ourselves); work (whether too much or too little); pride (in several directions); and the capacity to manipulate Scripture. He also makes several helpful suggestions for the priorities of those whose ministry vocation is academic writing.

Biblical studies can be dominated by a 'lust for mastery'. But we also learn Scripture's great antidote: to practise the same humility *as was embodied by our Master.*

In the United Kingdom and in countries heavily influenced by British usage (such as Australia), 'theology' is a large category that includes biblical studies, historical theology, systematic theology, and much more. The 'trials of theology' are then the trials encountered in any of the disciplines covered by the large label 'theology'. This usage is worth recognizing, for in America and in countries heavily influenced by American usage (such as Canada), 'theology' is a narrower category, usually referring to systematic theology. Because this chapter on biblical studies is included in a book on the trials of theology, clearly the former usage prevails here: students in biblical studies – devoting years to studying the Old Testament or the New Testament – face a variety of challenges that need to be thought through and understood. As for the word 'trials', I take it to include not only the elements that make competence in biblical studies hard work, but also those elements that constitute temptations to sin. True, these are trials of rather different kinds, but perhaps not so distinct as one might first think, as we shall see.

For convenience, I shall group these trials into various domains.

Integration

Many have observed that with the astonishing multiplication of knowledge that has taken place during the last two or three centuries, genuine 'renaissance thinkers' – people who are competent and integrative across numerous fields – can no longer be found. This is true even *within* disciplines. One no longer studies physics; rather, one studies the properties of a postulated quark whose half-life is measured in nanoseconds. One no longer studies biology; rather, one devotes years in the sub-discipline of microbiology to reactions at the molecular level within particular cells. Similarly, within biblical studies there are few who study the Bible; rather, one writes a learned tome on one facet of pentateuchal criticism, on the theology of Haggai, on cognate Semitic idioms; one specializes in some facet of the synoptic problem, on the use of the Old Testament in Hebrews, on the significance of *pistis Christou*, 'the faith of Christ', in current debates on the new perspective on Paul. As the old adage puts it, we learn more and more about less and less.

Yet certain forms of integration are essential if a biblical theologian is to be mature. I shall mention four:

1. The need for the first is uncovered by most first-year theological students who arrive at Bible colleges and seminaries with a passionate delight in reading the Bible – and then after a few weeks stumble into things like Greek morphology, English-Bible content quizzes, and the demands of hermeneutics. They can end up with two mutually exclusive ways of reading Scripture. In the one, they apply all the critical tools they are learning and attempt an 'objective' study; in the other, they read the Bible divorced from such critical thought, for they are having their 'devotions' and simply want God to speak to them personally and in an edifying fashion as he seemed to do before this wretched course in theological study was undertaken. This polarization of reading approaches is to be resisted as an abomination. In your most diligent technical study, you should be trying to understand what God himself has said through this text, trying to think God's thoughts after him, worshiping God with reverence and joy as you deploy your newly learned 'tools' to think more critically. (The word 'critically' in this context, of course, does not mean you 'criticize' the Bible or its contents, but that you seek justification and reasons for every interpretation you adopt.) And

when you read the Bible in quietness, not for any course assignment but 'devotionally', you should be observant, careful, 'critical' in the best sense, eager to learn, to see connections. Sometimes you will be impelled, even while thinking through and praying over a text, to pull a commentary or two off a shelf to make sure you are understanding the biblical passage responsibly.

2. More broadly, theological students, like the ministers many of them aspire to be, should aim not only to be learned (for being learned is a prerequisite for being qualified to teach) but also to be godly. There must be an integration of knowing what texts mean, and following them; of learning what Scripture says about the cross of Christ, and applying it to one's own life; of absorbing the biblical emphases on, say, holiness and love, and becoming holy and loving. That presupposes love for Christ within the context of the Christian community; it presupposes relationships, some suffering, growth in reliance on God's providence and grace. What shall it profit biblical scholars to become experts on Greek aspect theory and on the relationship between Jude and 2 Peter, and lose their own souls? You can become an expert in number theory or plate tectonics without your discipline making any demand on you other than hard work and integrity. But the disciplines bound up with biblical studies bring a further urgent demand: you are studying the Word of God, and unless your study is integrated with faith, obedience, godliness, prayer, conformity to Christ,

rising love for God and for his image-bearers, you are horribly abusing the very texts you claim you are studying.

3. It is essential to work hard at integrating the texts you are currently studying into your understanding of the Bible as a whole. Only rarely do beginning theological students fail in this regard: the diversity of the course work prohibits them from focusing too narrowly. Ministers more commonly fall short in this area when they focus all their attention on short books, or on the epistles, or on the New Testament, and fail to learn how to teach and preach the whole counsel of God. But the worst offenders are frequently the biblical scholars who devote all their energy to one or two or a handful of parts of the Bible, and actually stop reading the rest of it. They do not discipline themselves to continue with accurate exegesis and theological reflection across the entire canon. They may remain broadly orthodox while losing all capacity to articulate how the current text ought to find its place in an integrated complexity that reasons its way to the gospel, to Christ, to the sweep of redemptive history that rushes toward Christ, his cross, resurrection, and ascension, and on to the new heaven and the new earth.

4. It is no part of wisdom to despise adjacent disciplines – systematic theology, historical theology, philosophical theology, various forms of biblical theology. Obviously, these disciplines have lessons to learn from careful and learned exegesis of the

sacred text; equally obviously, anyone who wrestles with the exegesis of a text should avoid thinking that they are a 'blank slate' as they approach it. They should carefully weigh interpretations of texts advanced in earlier ages, and learn from the creative integrations offered by other theologians. That means spending at least some time reading broadly in the fields of historical and systematic theology. One could adduce other disciplines (e.g. works on literature and literary genres). Time taken away from biblical studies and devoted to such adjacent disciplines will on the long haul pay huge dividends.

The first domain, then, where the demands of responsible biblical studies become part of the trials of theology, lies in various challenges of integration.

Work

Polar temptations lurk in this domain. On the one hand, the field of biblical studies is so large that the diligent and the industrious may be tempted to work themselves to exhaustion. Those learning the biblical languages will also want some degree of mastery of the cognates. Especially in the case of Hebrew, there are a lot of them (Ugaritic, old Egyptian and other cuneiform texts, Akkadian, Aramaic, languages related to the Babylonian and Persian empires; and so forth). Those studying the New Testament must learn not only Greek, but at least some Hebrew and Aramaic (since the New Testament quotes or alludes to the Old so often), and, if there is any desire to engage in serious textual criticism, Syriac, Latin, and Coptic. If one's theological study is in preparation for pastoral ministry, the language requirements are not so massive, but those who are responsible to teach and preach the Bible should make a valiant effort to gain some mastery of the biblical languages. Nowadays that should also include an introductory grasp of linguistics.

While we engage in exegesis of the biblical texts, we should become informed of the conclusions of earlier generations of interpreters of the Bible. Some knowledge of the history of interpretation is a necessity for students of biblical studies, not merely a happy option. But thoughtful preachers and teachers will want more than the history of interpretation. They will also want to avoid merely atomistic exegesis (note the comments on integration, above) – and the alternatives mean we have some responsibility to learn and interact with systems of thought. Good exegesis is more than parsing Greek, of course. Soon we find ourselves wrestling with different literary genres and assorted rhetorical devices. I have not yet mentioned the vast array of secondary sources that reflect contemporary discussion: how much we want to burrow into such material will depend on our intended audience.

If, then, we are by temperament somewhat perfectionist, it is not difficult, with such a vast array of data-rich fields before us, to become workaholics. And a true workaholic is unlikely to be a good spouse, a godly and wise parent, a faithful Christian. Work, intrinsically a good thing, easily becomes an idol.[1]

On the other hand, biblical studies, strange to say, can become a field where lazy students hide. They never do stellar work, but they get by. If they become pastors, they may put in long hours, but they will be ineffective hours because they

---

1. See Timothy Keller's recent book, *Counterfeit Gods* (New York: Dutton, 2009).

diddle away their time in lazy reading, endless visits to blogs, last-minute preparation, and sloppy work habits. Instead of really growing in life *and doctrine* [1 Tim 4:14-16], they decide that they studied theology while at seminary, and now they can read other things. ('I learned it,' one remarkably naïve man told me; 'I don't need to keep reading that stuff now.') A seminary education must never be viewed as a ticket to a job. It is the beginning of a lifetime of study and reflection, worked out in the hurly-burly of ministry. Most ministers do not have someone immediately over them to check up on how effectively they have used their time, how honestly they fill their hours. Thus the very posts that may feed the workaholic may be safe-havens for the lazy or ill-disciplined.

Pride

This domain has many facets. I shall mention five.

1. The desire to be admired and recognized runs deep in all of us. The line between godly affirmation and encouragement, on the one hand, and the lust to be number one (like Demetrius in 3 John), on the other hand, is never as sharply demarcated as we might like, because our motives are frequently mixed. The lust for recognition can attack theology students, pastors, and seminary teachers alike.

2. A peculiar form of pride may be located in our sheer enjoyment of discovery as we work through texts, write essays or books, and prepare sermons and lectures. Those who work in other disciplines may enjoy their work and discoveries just as much as we enjoy ours. The difference, of course, is that microbiologists and Shakespeare scholars are unlikely to think they are entitled to a high place in the spiritual

sphere because they have unravelled an arcane point within their disciplines. They may be exhilarated by their discoveries, but they are unlikely to think that because of these discoveries they are spiritually superior. But that is the kind of temptation we face. We exult in mastery of certain texts, but because those texts are the texts of Scripture, we think our mastery confers on us a more profound knowledge of God. We do not always recognize that the mark of true growth in the study of Scripture is not so much that we become masters of the text as that we are mastered by the text.

3. A subset of this pride in specialist biblical knowledge lurks behind the academic biblical specialists who think their sphere of competence qualifies them to be superior pastors. I hasten to add that many academic Bible teachers *are* so equipped, not least because not a few of them have at some point been pastors and missionaries themselves. But many *think* they are so equipped even though they are not. Their shortfall is not necessarily in the realm of people skills; rather, it has to do with orientation. College and seminary teachers deal almost exclusively with students who come to learn; pastors deal with a much wider diversity of ages, academic backgrounds, and degrees of hunger to learn the Scriptures. College and seminary teachers are inevitably drawn to new ideas, even while, if they are teaching in confessional schools, they recognize their responsibility to be faithful to those standards; pastors know they have a huge responsibility to nurture and protect God's

flock, to teach their brothers and sisters in Christ to be faithful, even while they have some interest in keeping abreast of trends so that they can be better pastors. College and seminary teachers do not usually engage in much evangelism; pastors who are faithfully doing their job are interacting constantly with unbelievers and are much concerned to lead lost men and women to Christ.

If those distinctions in orientation between, on the one hand, college and seminary teachers, and, on the other hand, pastors, are maintained for two or three decades, they may become acute differences in emphasis. What makes them especially dangerous to the academics is that, *precisely because of their expertise in the biblical texts*, they may not perceive their own dangers. After all, biblical experts are sometimes asked to speak at conferences for pastors; by contrast, unless they are specialists themselves, pastors are not invited to address professional society meetings of academics. The relationship between the two sides is tilted in favour of the biblical experts. Unless they have the hearts, the experience, and the commitments of pastors, they can quietly inflict a fair bit of damage on the people they train, all the while supposing that even if they are not currently serving as pastors they have the academic training that would make them superior pastors.

4. A great deal of pride turns on our standards of comparison. When we begin biblical studies, almost everyone knows more than we do, save other first-year students, some of whom do not achieve grades as good as ours. Pretty soon we are third-

year students or research students, and then there are many who cannot quite match our standards. Eventually we enter into a life of ministry in, say, the local church or a Bible college, where virtually no one whom we teach knows as much about the Bible as we do. Occasionally, of course, we mingle with other pastors, some of whom are far more astute than we are, or we attend professional meetings of biblical scholars where we come across minds so amazingly capacious that our limitations become a little clearer. Most of our ministry, however, is discharged in contexts that encourage us to think of ourselves as more knowledgeable about the Bible than others (which is true) and therefore superior (which is not). We forget Paul's rhetorical questions: 'What do you have that you did not receive? And if you did receive it, why do you boast as though you did not?' [1 Cor. 4:7].

So often it is the little things that betray us. Because, relative to others, we become knowledge experts (at least in the biblical arena), we may begin to act as if data are everything and relationships are of marginal significance. For those so inclined, study and books are a lot more attractive than people and pastoral problems; indeed, because the book that is our chief study is the Bible, we may actually justify our callousness towards people by claiming the priority of the study of the Bible, when a little self-examination suggests that at least in part we are pursuing our preferences.

5.   Under this 'Pride' domain, I have so far mentioned areas in which theologians, not least in biblical

studies, may descend to a variety of forms of arrogance. But sinful motives are so complex that not infrequently they are inverted. Many theologians, including students, ministers, and academic biblical experts, may actually feel threatened by 'lay' people they meet, each with their own guild of competencies: lawyers, doctors, accountants, CEOs, assorted scientists, wealthy business leaders, skilled professionals. The theologian knows that at least some of these people do not think that theologians have 'real' jobs. The subject matter is often regarded as ethereal; certainly their salaries are lower. Masking our insecurities and secret jealousies, pride may then erupt in an inverted form that makes free and easy human intercourse almost impossible, even with fellow believers.

Both kinds of pride belong to the still larger category of *self-justification*. That sin goes back to the Garden, where Adam blames Eve and Eve blames Satan himself. It is difficult to think of any sin we commit that does not include a dollop of self-justification. Jesus tells the parable of the Good Samaritan to a lawyer who asked a question because he 'wanted to justify himself' [Luke 10:29]. Elsewhere he condemns the Pharisees because, he says, 'You are the ones who justify yourselves in the eyes of others, but God knows your hearts. What people value highly is detestable in God's sight' [Luke 16:14-15]. The difference between the Pharisee and the tax collector lay in the fact that only one of the two was confident in his own righteousness [Luke 18:9]. In other words, self-justification wears many faces. Like the lawyer in Luke 10, it may ask a slightly stupid and certainly morally vacuous question because one's personal limitations have been exposed and one is trying to claw one's way back to the top. Like the Pharisee in Luke 18, it may pray with utterly unself-conscious arrogance and condescension. Like those in Luke 16, it may prefer the approval of fellow human beings much more than the approval of God. The common ingredient, self-justification, similarly lurks behind so many of our sins of pride, inverted or otherwise. And the biblical answer to *self*-justification, of course, is the justification we must have from outside ourselves, the justification only God can give. The more we succumb to the assorted convolutions fed by self-justification, the more our lives testify that we have not absorbed very well what it means to stand wholly justified before God on the sole ground of what Christ Jesus has borne on our behalf.

Manipulation of Scripture

All of us have witnessed some pretty amazingly ridiculous interpretations of Scripture, undertaken by well-meaning folk who are not much used to disciplined reading of *any* texts. When biblical scholars engage in the same game, of course, our tools are much more sophisticated. But make no mistake: many of us really do continue to play the game.

The pressures come from many quarters. On the right, we may want to come up with 'safe' exegeses that reinforce the biases of our own confessional group. After all, we will gain in influence and authority within that group if we maintain the stances of the group's elders. Interpretations that justify all the details of one's heritage are likely to be received with approval by the leaders of that heritage. On the left, the pressure to be seen to be academically respectable may push some of us towards exegetical conclusions that are in line with the kosher academic orthodoxies of our day, divorced from any sense of a heritage of confessionalism. Especially attractive for some is the deployment of newly developing literary 'tools' that promise insights that no one has ever had in the history of the church. Both of these pressures, of course, have to do with our own identities within particular groups, whether of the right or the left.

For others of us, cut from more nonconformist cloth, the temptation to come up with independent conclusions on just about everything is more appealing. We glory in our 'creative' approaches and interpretations, maintaining scant regard for two millennia of work done before us. Still others of us focus so strongly on *Wirkungsgeschichte* that we never have to decide anything: that is, we are so interested in the history of the interpretation of particular passages or books, carefully sifting every exegetical byroad, that our main point seems to be that there have always been great diversities of interpretations, so let's not get too excited about any one interpretative tradition, and let's be very careful not to say that any one of them is right and that others are correspondingly wrong.

If I were to begin to flesh out examples to illustrate these various interpretative temptations, this essay would immediately triple in length. But my main point here is simple: those who are well-trained in exegesis and hermeneutics are more capable than most in finding evidence and aligning it in such a way that the 'right' answer comes out. Being better trained in exegesis, including the background knowledge acquired in a lifetime in biblical studies, does not guarantee faithful interpretations. It may enable us to justify particularly 'clever' interpretations.

What is needed is the integrity that genuinely and patiently 'listens' to the text. This is not easy, often because of weaknesses that are polar opposites.

1. On the one hand, those who are prone to 'clever' interpretations that are highly creative may nurture very little regard for those that have come before. They might benefit from learning a bit more about the history of interpretation. More importantly, they need to bear in mind Paul's exhortation to Timothy: 'What you have heard from me, keep as *the pattern of sound teaching*, with faith and love in Christ Jesus. Guard the good deposit that was entrusted to you – guard it with the help of the Holy Spirit who lives in us' [2 Tim 1:13-14]. In other words, the Bible is not made up of discrete clever bits that can legitimately be slapped together any which way; rather, there is a *pattern* to the Bible's 'sound teaching' that must be patiently teased out, a pattern that then constitutes a sort of grid to screen out the least credible bits of imaginative innovation that would destroy that pattern. After all, Jehovah's Witnesses have the same Bible we do; moreover, they operate with a high doctrine of Scripture's authority, even though the *pattern* they find in the Scripture is very different from that of historic confessional Christianity. Of course, everyone concedes that patterns can be bad, and that bad patterns have to be ruled out by careful and detailed exegesis of text after text. My point, however, is more focused. All of us think we discern patterns of thought in the Scripture, but Paul insists that not all patterns are equal. He wants to encourage Timothy to adopt a particular pattern of 'sound teaching,' and today's interpreters should endeavour to follow the same course.

2. On the other hand, theologians may judge that the pattern they adopt, whether from the right or the left, *is* a sound pattern. They will then find reasons to manipulate the text being studied into the pattern already adopted. Thus the very virtue advocated under the first of these opposite weaknesses – that is, avoiding atomistic and clever exegeses by making reference to a larger pattern – now becomes a vice under this second – viz., allowing the *pattern* to enjoy such control, that texts are manipulated for exactly the *opposite* reason.

I do not see any infallible escape route from this pair of challenges. There is no decisive key or hermeneutical trick that enables us to walk unscathed between this Scylla and Charybdis. But a humble mind, learning from the past without being chained to the past, persistent prayer for the illuminating work of the Holy Spirit, willingness to talk things over with others of greater experience and skill, willingness to be corrected, a passionate desire to bring glory to God by representing what he says faithfully, living within the context of a local church – all these disciplines and graces contribute towards encouraging those in biblical studies to avoid manipulation of biblical texts.

Priorities

Those in biblical studies who go on to engage in a ministry of serious writing require some attention, because another array of challenges spring from a barrage of choices that must be made by them. These can be grouped into three foci:

1. What subjects should I tackle? What projects should I take on? Do I want my projects dictated by publishers who offer me contracts to do this or that? Or do I accept such assignments with considerable reserve in order to preserve a place for projects that I want to do because I think they are important or because I am interested in them, even though I do not (yet!) have a contract for them? What part of my study and writing time should be devoted to 'answering' positions with which I disagree, as opposed to writing positive expositions? Should I choose something on Old Testament or New Testament 'introduction,' as opposed to commentary or biblical theology? What place should I devote to editing volumes written by others?

There are no 'one-size-fits-all' answers to such questions. It is not so much a matter of good choices and bad choices, as a matter of choices and entailments. Which entailments an individual scholar might prefer will often depend on highly individual gifts. Some scholars, such as Colin Hemer, are utterly superb when it comes to wrestling with Greco-Roman and archaeological sources that serve to flesh out the New Testament, but by instinct, preference and training, they are unlikely to focus much attention on, say, the writing of standard commentaries or on the literature of Second Temple Judaism and its bearing on New Testament interpretation. Some scholars, such as Donald Guthrie, devote their entire careers to one domain, in his case New Testament introduction. Some will be Pauline scholars, or Johannine scholars, all their lives, and refuse to write

outside their chosen specialisms. Few will demonstrate mastery across a wide spectrum.

At most it is possible to give a few hints as to how
to address these kinds of questions. All things being
equal (as they rarely are!), if you can write material
at the top rank of scholarship and at a more popular
level, attempt both – and do not let the latter
devour the former. Try not to develop a reputation
for responding to everyone while writing little
that is positive; on the other hand, when you are
in a position to provide a strategic response to an
egregious trend, it may be the mark of elementary
Christian discipleship to take on the project. If you
develop a heart for a couple of big research and
writing projects, do not let all the little writing
demands and offers deter you from your vision.

2. For whom am I writing? For scholars? Pastors? The
    well-read layperson? For unbelievers? For students?
    At what level am I trying to pitch my piece? How
    much of my time should I devote to relatively
    ephemeral pieces (not least blogs) that may achieve
    comparatively wide circulation but that will not
    last long in public memory, over against major
    books that are read by far fewer people than are
    blogs, but which may be consulted for generations
    and, in the best cases, help to shape the direction
    of entire disciplines? It may take you three or four
    years to write a book that is published in Society
    for New Testament Studies Monograph Series or
    in Supplements to *Vetus Testamentum*, and then you
    discover that the publishers print and sell only about

a thousand copies, most of which are bought by libraries. On the other hand, that work may become the seedbed of decades of other work, cited by generations of commentary writers.

Once again there is no formula that will decide what course is best. Much depends on gift and grace and calling. But your choices will affect your vocabulary as you write, your footnoting, your use of technical terms, your choice of publisher, how explicitly and immediately edifying you try to be, and so forth.

3. How can I avoid a 'lone ranger' complex in my writing – a complex that can lead, on the one hand, to discouragement and despair; and on the other, ironically, to unmitigated arrogance? What choices should I be making to ward off these dangers?

Writing is an essentially lonely business – or, more accurately, it is an essentially alone business. Much of it has to be done alone (whether or not one feels lonely). This easily breeds many distortions in perception. Most doctoral students in biblical studies, for example, even the most emotionally stable of them, oscillate between thinking that their work is the greatest piece of theological reflection since at least Calvin, and being convinced that if doctoral degrees are handed out for rubbish of this order, then the degree cannot be worth much. Transparently both perceptions cannot simultaneously be true; usually neither is. But what can be done to damp down these oscillations? More importantly, how can the actual product, the writing itself, be improved by avoiding the 'lone ranger' syndrome?

The ideal, of course, is to work in collaboration. This does not necessarily mean that you have co-writers for a particular essay or book. It means, rather, that you develop friends, students, and colleagues with whom you share your work, and whose work you share. This may take the form of semi-formal discussion (such as 'The Inklings', that circle of friends around C.S. Lewis); or getting your doctoral students to read and critique your work; or at very least, having informal discussions with colleagues about the approaches and arguments you are adopting. Very often, and especially if you are writing in domains that do not fall within your primary areas of expertise, you are well advised to ask friends with more expertise than you enjoy in those areas to read and critique your work before it goes to press. It is far better to receive such criticism at that point than in reviews. Be sure to find some readers who will take stances quite different from yours: they are the ones from whom you are likely to learn the most. This also means, of course, that you will occasionally help other colleagues reciprocally.

Concluding reflections

Scanning this brief list of domains that generate trials for those engaged in biblical studies – whether 'trials' in the sense of difficulties, or 'trials' in the sense of temptations – I am struck by how interrelated they are. And as an antidote, one recalls the words of Calvin:

> I have always been exceedingly delighted with the words of Chrysostom, 'The foundation of our philosophy is humility;' and still more with those of Augustine,

'As the orator, when asked, What is the first precept in eloquence? answered, Delivery: What is the second? Delivery: What is the third? Delivery: so, if you ask me in regard to the precepts of the Christian Religion, I will answer, first, second, and third, Humility.'[2]

Such humility will teach us the inestimable privilege accorded to those of us who are free to devote many hours each week in studying God's gracious self-disclosure in holy Scripture, learning to think God's thoughts after him, working carefully and patiently through words breathed out by God himself (however mediated through highly diverse human writers) that we may better know him and his ways, and above all that we may better know the Word incarnate. The more we revel in the sheer joy of this privilege, the less will we succumb to the trials of biblical studies, and the more will we sing the new song of those who have been redeemed by the Lamb; the less will we be seduced by the lust for mastery, and the more will we delight in him who is Master of all.

---

2. Calvin, *Institutes* II.ii.11. I am grateful to Nathan Busenitz and Andy Naselli for drawing my attention to this passage.

9

The Trials of Church History

Carl R. Trueman

The study of theology may be a 'dangerous business' – but what could possibly be dangerous about church history!? Surely it is tame by comparison. Why then a chapter on its 'trials'?

Dr Carl Trueman, Professor of Historical Theology and Church History at Westminster Theological Seminary in Philadelphia, recognises that for most theological students this subject seems quite 'safe' because it seems irrelevant. But he tours us through some insidious errors that this subject can convey to us – and along the way, he also helpfully explains the best way to think about the purposes and practices of church history.

In a reflection on his personal journey in this field, we begin to see how limited human creatures can be enabled and stabilised in the gospel's truth, through the study of how others have handled it in the past.

The 'safety' of 'irrelevance'

If there are two things about which one can be almost certain in the world of theological education it is these: first, no-one comes to seminary, Bible college, or a university theology department in order to study church history; and, second, church history is regarded as a far safer subject for study in such environments than systematic or biblical studies.

As to the first, most students embarking on theological study do so because they want to understand God better; and the best way to do that would seem to be through study of the Bible and of systematic theology. Church history, often seen as little more than the study of names, dates and timelines, is a necessary evil, something which must be done in order to fill up the requisite number of credits on the degree course, not something which can in itself really contribute to the students' main goal. Indeed I remember the start of an academic year at Westminster, when a senior colleague gave an introduction of the curriculum to new students. He had projected onto the screen a diagrammatic representation of how the different disciplines connected to each other, and how the curriculum was meant to exhibit coherence, unity, and disciplinary symbiosis. As he talked through the chart, however, he suddenly realised that church history was in the bottom left corner, with no lines connecting it to any of the other subjects. There it was, in splendid isolation, unhindered by any link to theology, exegesis, or church praxis. That he happened to be a church historian himself merely enhanced the absurdist humour of the situation and served to reinforce the prejudices against church history which the new students had no doubt brought with them that day.

As to the second point – the perceived safeness of church history – this is surely a function of the first point. As it stands in somewhat embarrassing non-connection to the other disciplines, it can be pursued without having any adverse impact upon them. After all, if it is irrelevant, while it can do no good it can also do no harm. While study of the Bible throws up text-critical questions and problems relating to the miraculous; and while systematic theology might challenge students on various fronts (such as the old chestnut concerning how such a particular thing as the Incarnation can have universal significance across time and space); and while ethics might raise the spectre of, say, moral relativism – what can *history* do that is at all risky or dangerous? Whether John Calvin died in his bed or in his armchair is scarcely likely to impact one's view of the substance of the Christian faith.

Given these common perceptions of church history, I want to begin this essay on the potential dangers and pitfalls of the subject by recounting, in brief compass, the strengths of the discipline. After all, if church history's bland safety is a function of its perceived irrelevance, so it will first be necessary to disabuse the reader of this notion before we can really understand and thus get to grips with the risks it contains. Only once we understand how it is to function within the theological curriculum can we grasp the dangers which it brings in its wake.

While there are numerous benefits to studying church history (not least the interdisciplinary nature of the subject), I want to focus on two of the subject's particular strengths.

The first relates to the nature of Christianity. Put simply, Christianity is not invented afresh every Sunday but what is read, sung, preached, and prayed in churches around the world stands within an established tradition; and church history allows us to understand how that tradition has come to take the form it has.

Take, for example, the language of Trinity with which typical believers will be familiar. Typically, Trinitarian language speaks of God as three persons, one substance. Such terminology is not specifically biblical, but the church has universally come to regard the terms as encapsulating important biblical concepts. Why has it done this? Why has the church come to use language which is not found in the

Bible to express this important truth? Well, the answer is that the language is rooted in the creed approved by the church at the Council of Constantinople in 381; and the reasons why this creed has the form and terminology which it does have can only be fully appreciated when the various debates and discussions about what exactly the Bible taught about God's being and nature have been examined. In other words, a knowledge of church history can help us to understand why things which in themselves seem perhaps a little pedantic, or obscure, are actually very important elements of the faith of anyone who claims to take the Bible seriously.

The same applies to other church formulations. Why is it important to hold that Christ is one person, two natures? Why do Protestants hold to justification by the imputation of Christ's righteousness through faith? The doctrines themselves, bluntly stated, can sometimes seem abstract and irrelevant; but when they are set in the context of the church's history and life, their true significance and the reasons why they have been formulated in the way they have, all become apparent

A second important reason for studying church history is the perspective it gives on the present day church. One of the amazing things I discovered when I moved to the United States was that I not only had a perspective on American life which made it easier for me, as an outsider, to see distinctive elements of the culture, but that I also came to have a better grasp on the British culture I had left behind. Living in America, I suddenly came to realise that things with which I had grown up, and which I thought were simply universal aspects of human civilisation, such as decent cups of tea and commercial-free television, were actually distinctive parts of British culture and not aspects of nature after all. As the goldfish cannot sense the water in which it swims, so we all swim unknowingly in our own cultural waters; it is only as we move out of our own cultural comfort zone that we come to learn such things.

Studying history is thus like emigration or extended foreign travel, only cheaper and generally less inconvenient. It gives the student the opportunity to visit another time, another place, another culture; and in so doing the student (hopefully) becomes more aware of how the particulars of geographical and chronological location come to shape and influence the way people think. Thus at a time when 'contextualisation' is a popular contemporary cliché and shibboleth, history should really be coming into its own: study of contexts is, after all, something that historians have done for centuries. Indeed far from being the cutting-edge activity that so many assume it to be, 'contextualisation' is taken for granted by historians and scarcely thought worthy of special comment.

Given these strengths, however, we can now turn our attention to the dangers inherent in the discipline. For far from being the 'safe' subject, church history can present a series of challenges to Christian students of which they should be aware.

Hagiography and idealism
The first danger is perhaps the most obvious: hagiography. Essentially, hagiography involves an idealised view of the history of the church which refuses to acknowledge that even the greatest heroes of the faith, or the most important events, are always more or less flawed.

Hagiography has been around for as long as church history itself. In the second century, the account of the martyrdom of Polycarp, Bishop of Smyrna, presents a highly idealised picture of an old man going to be burned at the stake with joy, confidence, and fortitude, surrounded by evil and scheming enemies. Now, it is quite possible that Polycarp did die a very brave death more or less as the anonymous writer describes; but the presentation of his last days is so uniformly laudatory of him that the reader has to wonder if the person being described is a human being or rather some higher, almost divine individual who is unaffected by the emotions we might associate with impending death, such as fear and trepidation about the pain, even if he had no doubts about his eternal destination.

The same is also true with Athanasius's influential book, *The Life of Anthony*, which describes the amazing life, miracles and teachings of a third/fourth-century leader of the church, renowned for his life of rigorous asceticism in the desert. Again, the reader can often be left wondering if Anthony is a real man, given his lack of any internal struggle. He seems less a real human being and more of a cardboard cut-out or a two-dimensional character from a children's comic.

Hagiography has continued throughout the history of the church, through medieval accounts of saints to Reformation stories of martyrdom down to the present day, when a myriad of popular Christian books often portrays our heroes as just that: heroic figures of a different order to the rest of us. Like so many Greek icons, such books present us not with human beings as they are, but human beings as we think they should be.

The issue of hagiography also bleeds over into idealism. We can sometimes have a tendency to view events in church history through rose-tinted spectacles. One classic example is the Council of Nicaea in 325, which moved discussion of the doctrine of God in a very positive direction towards the establishment of Trinitarianism as basic to the church's confession. By all accounts, this was a great achievement, and one for which Christians should be grateful. But the Council was also tied up with the politics of the empire and the machinations and ambitions of the Emperor Constantine. Orthodoxy did not win simply by being the truth; there was a lot of political chicanery involved as well. This does not invalidate the result (as I shall argue below) but it should alert us to the need to understand the event as being a little more complex than the result simply of a gathering of men who were passionate for the truth.

Now hagiography has its place in the church, not in the sense of telling exaggerated or plain false stories about great people and events in order to make them seem better than they really were, but in the sense of focusing on the strengths or the positive aspects of church history in order to provide encouragement for the reader. But such focus should always be done in conscious knowledge that human beings are flawed. The student should be particularly aware that, when writing an essay for a professor, the professor is not looking to see that the student understands that Luther or Nicaea or the Chalcedonian Definition were 'good things'. The professor also wants to see that the student understands the complicated and often morally murky forces which surrounded these historic people and entities, and out of which God brought good, despite the unpromising nature of the material with which He had to work.

In short, part of the answer to hagiography and a naïve idealism about church history is a robust understanding that all human beings, even our greatest heroes of the faith, are fallen; and that this fallenness profoundly shapes the way they act and think.

Historicism and relativism

If hagiography is one problem which has traditionally dogged history written by those with Christian commitments, another danger, more sophisticated perhaps and even more dangerous, is that of historicism and its concomitant relativism.

Historicism is a term used to describe a number of different approaches to history but, in essence, it refers to a tendency to so contextualise historical actions and events that their significance is effectively *isolated* in the past. As such, historicist approaches do embody an extremely important part of historical method: the setting of historical phenomena within their proper historical context. Where they err is in stressing this context to the point where the past is effectively isolated from any point of contact with the present.

As a good example of how contextualisation should properly proceed, we might point to the discussions of Martin Luther's attitude to the Jews in Europe. It is well-known that Luther wrote a polemical treatise in 1543, *On the Jews and Their Lies*, in which he attacked Judaism using the most violent language and incited his readers to go out and commit acts of murder against them. This treatise has often been used to make the case that Luther was violently anti-Semitic and to posit a direct connection between him, his teaching, and the atrocities of the Third Reich. William L. Shirer most famously made this case in his massive journalistic history of Nazism, *The Rise and Fall of the Third Reich* (1960).

There are numerous problems with this thesis, however. First, the term *anti-Semitism* is misleading because it presupposes a concept of 'race'. But their 'race' was not the problem Luther had with the Jews. He simply did not think in such a category; rather, it developed in the nineteenth century on the back of quasi-scientific theories of human origins. Luther may have hated the Jews, but he did so on religious grounds – they denied the Gospel – and not racial grounds. Thus, if any Jews converted to Christianity, they would not be a problem to him any more. If, however, a Jew in Berlin in the late 1930s had converted to Christianity, it would have made no difference: the Nuremberg laws made it clear that the problem was their race, not their religion.

Second, Luther is actually a very 'conventional' hater of the Jews: even the notorious treatise of 1543 uses standard propaganda of his day, such as the so-called 'blood libel', the idea that Jews would kidnap Christian children to crucify them. Thus, Luther's treatise, when compared to other similar documents of the time, looks anything but unique.

There is more that could be said on this point, but suffice to say that the setting of Luther's treatise in the wider cultural context immediately requires that we rethink any claims which connect it too directly to events in Nazi Germany: he thought in non-racial categories; and he was simply one voice among many that were saying the same thing. The connection of Nazism to Luther is thus far more complex than many have cared to make it.

In this example, historicism helps to relativise Luther in a good way, highlighting the fact that history is always more complicated than we might first imagine, and that the past (to use the now-clichéd phrase from L.P. Hartley) is a different country where people do things differently.

The danger, of course, is that historicism can be taken to such an extreme that the historian loses sight of any analogy or connection between the past and the present, and thus effectively reduces history to little more than a canvas on to which the historian can project his or her own politics and agenda, as merely one more arena where the battle of interpretations is played out in a manner where the one who shouts loudest (or has the most effective lobby group) is always the one who wins. Recent years have seen a veritable blossoming of such approaches, as every identity group insists on developing its own history: black, 'queer', feminist, post-imperialist: whatever identity politics we care to name, each now has its own 'history'.

We should even acknowledge that some of these approaches have yielded real insights. It is important to be made aware of the predominant points-of-view from which history has traditionally been written, and these 'counter histories' certainly act as healthy correctives to the excessive privileging of particular perspectives. Take for example the history of the British Empire. In the nineteenth century, it was seen by countless British (or perhaps, to be more specific, *English*) writers to be the meaning of history, the culmination of the development of the greatest nation on earth. However over the last sixty years historians have pointed out that this empire was not bought without cost, that there was terrible exploitation and bloodshed which undergirded it in many parts, and that significant parts were played in its development by women and by native populations. New histories have helped to show that the accounts given by the white males, who benefited the most from imperialism and who generally sat at the top of the political tree, did not represent the whole story. So far, so helpful.

The danger, however, is that history becomes reduced to a 'viewpoint', so that you have your truth about history and, frankly, I have mine. At its most extreme, this can render the historian impotent in the face of something as egregious and historically fallacious as Holocaust Denial. A statement such as 'Well, six million Jews dying in the Holocaust is merely your perspective on events', may sound bizarre to us; but unless one is prepared to argue for some level of objectivity in historical method, there is really no response to it.

For a Christian, the dangers may not be as obvious nor as extreme as those posed by a radically relativist approach to history confronted by Holocaust Denial, but they can still be significant. To return to the doctrine of the Trinity for example: any account of the events in the fourth century, leading up to the Council of Nicaea in 325 and then to the Council of Constantinople in 381, will involve some engagement with the wider context. That will require acknowledging that much of the debate was shaped by imperial politics; that protagonists on all sides of the debate acted at times with little integrity or honesty; that the story as we have it is refracted through texts which are written from particular viewpoints; and that women, the poor, and the illiterate, to name but three groups, are almost entirely absent from the sources we use and the accounts we write. The temptation, therefore, might be to say something akin to this: 'Well, the doctrine of the Trinity is simply a construct, put together by a group of men; thus, it represents at best the faith of a tiny, self-selected minority at the top of the social and intellectual hierarchy; further, there were various models of how to think about God which were available; this one just happened to strike a chord with the most powerful military and political factions, and it was this which guaranteed its success. In addition, this is a fourth-century issue; it has no relevance to the twenty-first century world in which we live.'

Such an approach makes a host of presuppositions. To take the last issue first (that of it being a fourth-century doctrine of no relevance to today): the presupposition is that there is no common ground between the fourth century and the present day which would allow for such relevance. Further, looking at the other objections, we can see several similar assumptions: that imperial politics and ecclesiastical sleaze were involved in the formulation of the doctrine of the Trinity, is taken to mean that the doctrine can be more or less reduced to such antics; that the group doing the defining were only a small minority and unrepresentative of society as a whole, is taken to mean that the doctrine is at best the speculation of a few, and at worst a means of imposing one group's views and power upon others.

History is messy, and the Christian who does history needs to acknowledge that. We have already noted that hagiography can be a most mischievous and problematic way of analysing the great events and personalities of the church's past. But it is also clear that the historicist avoidance of hagiography brings its own temptations.

A personal story

To engage for a moment in a brief autobiographical reflection, I well remember how, as a naïve conservative evangelical student in my first year of Ph.D. studies, I was shaken by the impact which the acknowledgement of context and contextualised human agency had on my understanding of the Reformation. It seemed irrefutable that Luther was shaped in part at least by his relationship with his father – who, after all, is not? – but where did that fact leave his doctrine of justification? Was it simply, as Erik Erikson argued, a projection of his own psychological struggles? And did this mean that all Christian doctrine might be reducible to the psychological pathologies or personal contexts of the particular theologians involved? A number of factors helped extricate me from the relativist morass into which I felt myself descending.

First, I realised that historical action is always complex, and, as such, can never be reduced to a single cause. This cuts both ways: while one should not naïvely reduce, say, the events surrounding the Council of Constantinople in 381 to the valiant, selfless, and pure desire of the orthodox party to honour God by simply expounding his word; neither should one reduce them to being merely the result of imperial politics, ecclesiastical manipulation or psychological quirks. This important point highlights the fact that in my chosen field of the history of doctrine, its *theological* element is not to be discounted simply because other factors also came in to play.

Second, I noticed that even given the vast geographical and temporal distance between myself and the objects of my study, there were actually a number of common factors between myself and those I studied. These allowed a kind of 'connection' between me, a British student in the 1980s, and Martin Luther, a German monk in the early sixteenth century. We shared common texts, for example: the Bible, Luther's writings, and the writings of those with whom he interacted throughout his life. (Of course, I was also assuming that texts do have meanings, a point which has itself been subject to vigorous criticism by philosophers who would rather see meaning as rooted in the reader or the reading community. Such a radical position seems to me flawed, and indeed deeply problematic, given that it flies in the face of how people actually *live* day to day: as an Academic Dean, I have never come across a reader-response advocate so radical that he does not believe his contract of employment does not have an intrinsic, non-negotiable meaning. This radical position is incoherent, given that it is a truth claim made using words. It is arguably also immoral, given that it both cedes all power to those who control how texts are read, and gives no basis for resisting readings of history such as those offered by Holocaust Deniers. And if you disagree with what I have written in this paragraph, I might respond by saying that such disagreement itself presupposes a meaning with which one disagrees.)

In my postgraduate musings about our connections, I also realised that Luther and I shared a common human nature. (Again, this is a point which has been vigorously repudiated by numerous postmodern philosophers; yet it seems to be a matter upon which most thinkers have agreed throughout history, whether basing such a belief in the Bible's teaching, upon Enlightenment notions of rationality, or on common sense of the kind which seems to acknowledge the biological fact that humans can reproduce with each other but not with members of other species, and so must have some kind of continuity with one another.)

To acknowledge the existence and unity of human nature meant that while our contexts were very different, I could yet look at Luther's writings – his linguistic actions, to use slightly more theoretical language – and come to understand how he was using language because the linguistic function of one human being is analogous to that of another, and thus the two are commensurable in some way. I may not be able to know every thought that passed through Luther's mind when he wrote, say, *The Ninety-Five Theses Against Indulgences* (1517), but through hard work and attention to context I could reconstruct much of what he was intending *to do* when he produced that particular work. I needed to research the genre of disputation theses; I needed to grasp some medieval theology; I needed to understand what was going on in and around Electoral Saxony in 1517; and I needed to be familiar with Luther's own life up to that point; but once I had a reasonable handle on each of these things, I could articulate a reasonable – though necessarily not exhaustive – account of what he was doing when he posted the *Ninety-Five Theses* on that fateful day in October, 1517.

This capacity for connection with him did not address the question of the extent to which Luther's teaching was *true*; and there is a sense in which that was not my concern. As a historian, I am generally preoccupied with 'why' questions relating to the *reasons* people acted the way they did, and thus not so much with issues relating to truth or falsity. What my reflections on complexity and human nature did, however, was to allow the possibility that what Luther said *might* be true, and *might* transcend the particulars of time and space. For a Christian, the truth or otherwise of any theological claim is to be established on the basis of criteria external to Luther's own texts and context – that is, upon God's word, the Bible. Contextualisation and complexity did not require that all truth claims became utterly relative.

I also learned to distinguish between *neutrality* and *objectivity*. Neutrality is impossible. Nobody can rise above all contexts in order to study history. Even as I write this, I am conscious that my own background and my own immediate circumstances are parts of who I am as a historian and shape the way I approach this subject. But to reject neutrality is not to reject objectivity. The historical profession is built upon a set of procedures of verification, laid down in some detail by the great German historian Von Ranke in the nineteenth century. These principles address ways of marshalling and analysing evidence. They reflect good historical method. Yet *interpretation* is different again: it involves the engagement of the philosophical assumptions of the historian with the evidence. The result is that historians of all different stripes – Marxists, Weberians, Hegelians, etc. – offer different interpretations of historical events but can nonetheless talk to each other and debate and fight over their different narratives and conclusions precisely because they share common procedures of verification. All good historians agree *that* the Holocaust really happened; but there may be various ways of understanding *why* it happened or *what it signified*. That their interpretations differ, and sometimes completely disagree, does not require that we regard every interpretation as equally valid.

Conclusion

My suspicion is that of all temptations currently facing students of church history, the temptations to historicism and relativism will be the most alluring. These are, after all, the very life-breath of so many of the trendy philosophies bandied about in university departments of humanities and literary theory. It is also, perhaps even more significantly, the temper of the times. One can scarcely switch on the television these days without the radical moral relativism of so much of the modern Western world pouring into one's living room from such intellectual giants as Oprah Winfrey and her various equivalents across the globe. We might scoff at the banality of these voices, but there is a constant-drip effect of the message that 'this is my truth and it works for me', particularly when combined with the assumption that we in today's world have outgrown the ideas and ideals of yesteryear. But this kind of teaching is like carbon monoxide: its effect is silent but deadly, and indiscernible until it is too late.

Thus, my final word on history would be this: every history student should purchase a few good books on how to do history. My own favourites are David Hackett Fischer's *Historians' Fallacies: Towards a logic of Historical Thought* (New York: Harper and Row, 1970); and Richard J. Evans' *In Defence of History* (London: Granta, 1997). The student who reads and mulls over these two books should be well-placed to handle many of the issues which the modern taste for radical relativism and historicism throw up. In addition, there is, of course, no substitute for reading good history. I read as much history as I can, always with a view not only to seeing what the historian is saying about the chosen subject but also to observe what they do with the relevant evidence. Reading a good historian in this manner is like watching a great artist paint a picture. Not all of us will be able to replicate the brilliance of the teacher, but all will find their own technique and ability somewhat improved as a result.

10

The Trials of Systematic Theology

Gerald L. Bray

Systematic theology is a way of thinking and talking about God, taking what is said about God throughout Scripture and knitting it together in a summary form. These summaries never stand above Scripture, but are attempts to distil Scripture into a more manageable package in order to aid our learning about God and discussions of him. This skill is non-negotiable for pastors, hence theological students are necessarily taught in systematics.

Revd Dr Gerald Bray, Research Professor at Samford University's Beeson Divinity School in Birmingham, Alabama, alerts us to some pitfalls in the study and practice of systematic theology. There are the twin dangers of abstraction and apostasy: it is easy to find systematicians who dispute the role and authority of Scripture, and many works of systematic theology claim to speak of God using other means. But Dr Bray goes on to show how the practice of systematic theology arises from the person of God, and how it is necessary for pastors, who all have to be theologians of sorts. He ends by giving some guidance for connecting the seeming abstractness of systematic theology with our lived experience of the God we seek to love.

The vices of theology: abstruseness and apostasy

There can be few subjects that cause greater trepidation in the minds of theological students than systematic theology, which sounds so abstract and forbidding. After all, we believe in a living God who acts in our lives, not in a geometric construct presented to us in incomprehensible diagrams. Life is more complex and varied than any theory, and we suspect that those who attempt to systematise it will do an inadequate job, and more than likely end up in heresy. The great systematicians all have their detractors as well as their followers, and none more so than Karl Barth (1886–1968) who by common consent is the greatest of them in recent times. At the same time, we have to recognise that there is also a minority of students for whom systematics is not frightening at all. On the contrary, for them it is the stuff of theology and they take to it in the way that a duck takes to water. Late-night discussions of supralapsarianism or annihilationism, replete with obscure quotations (preferably in Latin or German), energise them in a way that nothing else can. They are usually so caught up in what they are doing that they fail to see that they are alienating almost everyone else, confirming the fears of other people that systematic theology has no relationship to everyday life. Even worse, discussions of that kind can end up in heated arguments that are capable of destroying friendships and splitting fellowships over matters that only a few specialists understand. Do we really need this? What is the point of immersing oneself in a discipline, if it is likely to lead to false teaching or cause division in the church?

Systematic theology has a bad press and it is not surprising that many theological colleges do their best to avoid it. They call their courses in the subject 'Christian doctrine' and concentrate on specific topics, like the Trinity or Christology, or on the theology of some part of the Bible. What Luke or James said about God is a manageable topic and can be justified as 'biblical' without raising the philosophical questions that would force students to relate such material to universal concepts. Those who want to take matters further may be quietly dissuaded from doing so, perhaps on the grounds that it will take them away from the source of our knowledge of God in the Bible. Scripture contains many different kinds of writing, but systematic theology is not one of them, and so it is not difficult to suppose that the discipline has little to do with God's self-revelation in his eternal Word.

This impression is reinforced by the fact that systematic theology as we know it now did not appear until the Middle Ages. The first theologian who consciously tried to be systematic in his approach was John of Damascus (675–749) and it may be for that reason that he is generally regarded as the last of the ancient Greek fathers of the church. John summed up what had already been written by others, and did such a good job of it that nobody followed him. Even today, there are people in the Eastern churches who believe that his was (and still is) the last word on any given subject and that to go beyond him is to venture into dangerous territory. This of course is precisely what the Western church did, several centuries later, when its theologians developed theology as a discipline to be taught in the nascent universities of medieval Europe. Beginning with men like Peter Lombard (d. 1160) and continuing through to the great work of Thomas Aquinas (1226–1274) and his contemporaries, these 'scholastics' as they are now called, invented an academic discipline that consciously tried to organise everything we know about God. To be truly systematic it was necessary to offer a complete picture, with the result that the scholastic theologians found themselves debating such obscure topics as the nature of Christ's descent into hell and drawing fine lines of distinction between different types of sin, which led them to invent correspondingly different degrees of divine grace. They were not averse to speculating about matters that are not clearly revealed in Scripture, and their propensity to give elaborate answers to complicated and somewhat artificial questions has given scholasticism a bad name ever since.

The Protestant reformation rebelled against this kind of approach – but not as much as we might think. Men like Martin Luther (1483–1546) and John Calvin (1509–64) were brought up on Peter Lombard and so could hardly escape his influence, and their followers soon developed a form of Protestant scholasticism which came to define their theology. What we think of today as Lutheranism and Calvinism is essentially the result of this neo-scholasticism, which reaches us in the form of creedal statements like the Westminster Confession of Faith. Some people even claim that Anglicanism has produced a foundational systematic theologian in the person of Richard Hooker (1554–1600), although such a description of him is highly misleading. In modern times, systematic theology appears either as an exposition and defence of the established creeds and confessions of a particular denominational tradition, or else a conscious revolt against them in the name of some other principle. In the eighteenth century, that principle was often human reason, but things have moved on since then to embrace such diverse phenomena as religious 'feeling' and experience, history, psychology, social anthropology and even quantum physics. In the course of all this, the Bible has often been left behind, sometimes far behind, and it is not unusual for modern systematicians to reject large parts of it that do not correspond to their notions of what God is like. When this happens we are no longer dealing with divine revelation but with human perceptions of reality which are governed by the prejudices of our age as much as by anything else.

The result is that what passes as 'systematic theology' today is often anything but a genuine study of God and his purposes. It can even go to the opposite extreme and become an attempt to explain those away in the light of 'modern knowledge', whatever that is supposed to be.

Unfortunately, those who reject this way of thinking usually fall back on the classical formulations of the past and so run the risk of appearing irrelevant today. Even if there is nothing wrong with the Apostles' Creed or the Westminster Confession, to confine oneself to them is to leave out many of the questions that concern modern thinkers, particularly in the realm of ethics. If traditionalism is allowed to become archaism it discredits the heritage it is trying to preserve, and many who start out along those lines become so disillusioned by that approach that they slide – sometimes quite dramatically – towards the opposite end of the spectrum. We must not forget that some of the most liberal minds of our time started out in conservative, even in 'fundamentalist', circles and rejected them precisely because of their inadequacy in this area.

The biblical basis of systematics: 'One God'

Can systematic theology be saved? Can it be recommended as a valid and compelling discipline for students to embrace today? Is there anything in it besides heresy and unbelief at the end of the road? To answer these questions we must begin from the basic principles of God's self-revelation in Scripture.

Let us admit at the outset that the Bible is not presented to us as a theological textbook, or indeed as any kind of textbook. It is a composite work of many hands and styles which have to be evaluated and absorbed in different ways. Nevertheless, it holds together as a single collection of books because it has a basic theme that has not changed over time and space. For all their many differences, Abraham in the city of Ur and John on the island of Patmos shared a great many beliefs in common. Both of them had met the one living and eternal God, who revealed himself to them as he really is and directed them to act accordingly. Abraham left his home and family and set out on a journey that would take him to a country of which he knew nothing, but where his descendants would flourish and become a great nation. John wrote down the stupendous vision that he saw and probably only partly understood, but he knew that whatever the details of the final outcome might turn out to be, it would be the culmination and ultimate validation of the revelation given to Abraham at least two millennia before. John knew that the God who revealed himself on Patmos was the eternal I AM, the One who is and who was and who is to come, the Almighty. Everything else flows from that, and it is not possible to make any sense of the Apocalypse without a thorough knowledge of the tradition of revelation going right back to Ur of the Chaldees and beyond.

It is this basic truth which justifies the construction of a systematic theology. There is only one God and one Mind that has formed and executed the plan of human salvation which reached its climax in the life, death and resurrection of Jesus Christ and which awaits its final consummation in his return to judgment. The oneness of the Planner ensures the consistency and coherence of the Plan. To the objection that it is perfectly possible for a human planner to come up with incoherent and inconsistent plans, we have to say that the divine Planner is not limited by the sorts of handicap that make that possible – indeed, almost inevitable – in the case of human beings. Even if God were to do something that appears inconsistent and incoherent to us, it would not be so to him because the factors which would lead us to draw such a conclusion do not apply in his case.

If this sounds like some abstract theory, take a look at a concrete example and you will see what I mean. The Bible tells us that God loves his creatures and does not want any of them to perish. It also tells us that his rebellious human subjects must surrender to him and be born again in Christ – or perish is precisely what they will do. How is this possible? Is it not a contradiction to say that an all-powerful God allows his will to be thwarted? Theologians have wrestled with this question for hundreds of years. Some have concluded that God is not really all-powerful; but that is a heresy. Others have said that it is not really true to say that God does not want anyone to perish – those words have to be understood, we are told, not as a straightforward statement of fact but as a warning not to exclude people from the kingdom of God in advance simply because *we* have decided that they cannot be saved. Still others have concluded that God will not allow anyone to die eternally. According to them, the warning is there to remind us that we must take our lives seriously, but in the end God will rescue everybody.

But none of these interpreters have fully grasped the reality of God's self-revelation. It is undoubtedly true that we are faced with a paradox that is difficult, if not impossible, for human minds to resolve satisfactorily; but that does not mean that God is inconsistent or incoherent. Both truths have to be held together, and this is possible because the God we worship is greater than we are. His thoughts are high above our thoughts and cannot be reduced to them, however tempted we may be to do so. This does not mean that the work of the systematic theologian is useless, but that he must understand himself to be dealing with realities that go beyond the limitations of ordinary human logic yet are not irrational or unreasonable. God is love and as anyone who has experienced love will know, that is precisely what love is like – yet who would suggest that it should be discounted simply because we do not fully understand it? We enter into it and it makes sense; the task of the theologian, as of the poet, is to put that sense into words that come close to doing justice to it, even if we can never hope to exhaust the depths of the reality itself.

Near the beginning of the Bible, God declares, 'Hear, O Israel: The LORD our God, the LORD is one' [Deut. 6:4]. Toward the end of the Bible, the author to the Hebrews states that 'Jesus Christ is the same yesterday and today and for ever' [Heb. 13:8]. The theologian seeks to understand the unity, consistency and coherence of God's self-revelation, which is the fundamental justification for systematic theology. The first and main purpose of the discipline is evangelistic, because it aims to demonstrate to the unbelieving world that it is possible to believe in this God and accept his revelation without falling apart intellectually. The Mind who created us has given us minds to understand him and his works, at least to some degree, and that understanding is accurate and sensible within the parameters set by our Creator. The fact that there are many things we cannot know does not mean that there is nothing we can grasp; if that were so, revelation would be impossible and could not have happened. Defending the divine character of the Bible therefore necessitates a systematic theology. The sooner we recognise this, the better.

The pastor-theologian's purpose

But even if we accept that one God can be known across the Scriptures, why should theological students have to deal with such complexity? After all, the vast majority will go on to become pastors, not the kind of 'systematic theologian' who writes textbooks and articles. Not everyone who seeks to be a pastor has the kind of mind that can easily integrate all this scriptural material, or sieve through the writings of theologians. So why bother? What could possibly be the point of engaging in 'systematic theology'? Why not merely learn something of the Bible, and some 'practical' skills such as 'information technology for ministers' or 'pastoral counselling' or 'liturgical studies'?

Every pastor *needs* to be a 'pastor-theologian', because every Christian has a systematic theology of some kind. What theologians express is something that ordinary Christians keep to themselves and often cannot put into words – though they do quickly react when someone says something that goes against it. For example, let us say that an ordinary believer is accused of thinking that God is a big man in the sky, surrounded by little baby angels, whose greatest pleasure is to contemplate the torture of those whom he has condemned to everlasting damnation. The ordinary believer would almost certainly deny it, even if he could not explain why he thought such a picture was wrong. In fact there is plenty of Christian art supporting the picture painted by the sceptic; but it doesn't deter the true believer, who knows that such depictions do not correspond to the reality, even if he cannot say precisely what that reality is.

People like this – the vast majority of church members – have a feel for orthodoxy in such matters. But they need gifted thinkers and teachers to flesh it out for them, and this is where the pastor-theologian comes in, who in turn needs to learn from the systematic theologian. Systematic theology is not only evangelistic but also pastoral, helping to educate and build up the believer in his faith, so that he may have a better and more articulate understanding of his beliefs. If faith is in the heart, then we may think of the theologian as a kind of spiritual cardiologist, who examines the workings of the heart so that its secrets may be more fully understood. (But if the theologian starts to claim that he can understand those secrets in a way that ordinary people cannot; or he invents new 'truths', or discounts the existence of old truths, he has overstepped the mark and has ceased to function as his discipline demands. Those who seek the truth are valuable and necessary guides, but those who manipulate it are dangerous charlatans who must be avoided at all costs. This is why systematic theology is both the greatest and the most feared of the theological disciplines. All too often, its practitioners incline to one extreme or the other, and find it hard to stay on track.)

Medical imagery of the kind used here is helpful in understanding what role systematic theology plays in the life of a pastor. People who go to their doctor are not troubled by esoteric anatomical questions like: 'Why do I have one head and two legs instead of the other way round?' A few may wonder why they exist at all, but if so, they are unlikely to ask the doctor, since he will not know the answer either. Most of the people in the surgery waiting room are there because something they have always taken for granted has started to behave abnormally, and they want to know what can be done about it. The doctor has to figure out what is wrong and prescribe the appropriate treatment, which is often fairly routine but which may turn out to be quite complicated, and which can never be taken for granted.

Every person is different, and what works for one (or even for most) is not guaranteed to work for all.

Similarly a pastor usually confronts theological issues in terms of questions that arise, which may seem to have little to do with theology (on the surface at least). It is his task to work out what the underlying theological principles are, and then to find the right application to the circumstance in question, always remembering that each case is different and that simple answers, while useful some of the time, cannot be relied upon to work well in every situation.

In our modern world the questions that come up most often are ethical ones. The issue of homosexual practice is ultimately rooted in the doctrine of creation, and the answer to it depends on our understanding of what the sexes were made for. It becomes more subtle when its advocates start to argue that some people are created with a dominant same-sex attraction and should therefore be allowed to live out their inclination in the same way that heterosexually-oriented people do. Even if it is true that some people are made this way (and that is by no means certain), that is not enough for a theologian to acquiesce in the practice. Creation does not merely exist; it is there for a purpose, and sexual intercourse was intended to bond man and wife together in a state of lifelong monogamy. Anything other than that is a perversion of God's intentions, however 'natural' and justified it may seem to be on other grounds. Only clear-headed, systematic thinking can help us here. (Swapping Bible verses and/or personal experiences is not good enough.) People may not listen to our reasoning or accept it, but the same is true in medicine also – not everyone does what their doctor advises! That is not the point. A pastor must be faithful to the word of God, whether or not he likes it or others receive it.

Learning theology as pastors

The doctor in his surgery may not have to consult his medical handbooks, but he has to understand the principles of medicine sufficiently well to be able to give the right advice. Likewise, a pastor may not look everything up in some book of systematic theology lying close to hand, but he has to know enough about how it works to be able to tell his parishioners what God wants them to do. The systematic theologian may not be a gifted pastor, but he has to provide the underlying framework within which the answers given by the pastor make sense. Some systematicians may write in a way that is more user-friendly than others (though we have to admit that this can be a problem) but all have to bear in mind the fundamental truth that if their message cannot be preached, it is not good theology. Complexity may be unavoidable; but if it fades into obscurity, it can do no good and will end up bringing the entire discipline into disrepute.

Should a student of theology attempt to be systematic in his approach? The answer can only be 'yes'. Failure to embrace a coherent picture of God and his works can only produce confusion at the level of application, since it will be unclear to the pastor how it all hangs together and what parts of the system are most relevant to the case in hand. Too often what we see today is an emotional, off-the-cuff response to issues that arise, which shows that those concerned care passionately about the subject, but give no evidence that they have thought deeply about it or are capable of resolving the problem they are faced with. For that, a dispassionate and wide-ranging analysis is required, and that takes time and study. Only a man with a well-grounded systematic mindset is likely to be able to think the issues through deeply enough to be able to come up with a viable answer in the short time that is usually available to him. As ministers of the gospel well know, it is their knowledge of the basic theological principles that enables them to cut through to the heart of the matter and provide what others may think is an 'off-the-cuff' answer. Those without such specialist training are left floundering or, worse still, are subject to knee-jerk reactions that are almost bound to make the problem worse. The idea that all difficulties can be solved by prayer and the laying-on of hands is widespread today, but unless the problem was inconsequential to begin with, such methods are unlikely to bear much fruit. Too often what we see is that people with real problems become psychologically dependent on a pastor or a church and keep returning for more of the same sort of treatment, when a little practical counsel and spiritual direction rooted in fundamental principles could have solved the problem once and for all.

The difficulties of studying theology

So the pastor and the theologian have to be in constant communication with one another, so that the principles enunciated by the one can be properly assimilated by the other and preached to God's people in an effective way. But we must not pretend that the study of systematic theology is painless or that those who embark on it will have an easy time. As we have already seen, there is a temptation to react by simply regurgitating the formulas of the past without thinking them through. I have also admitted that not everyone has an aptitude for systematic thinking, and these people will have to work harder at this subject (just as others have to work harder at biblical languages or at learning to preach well). On the other end of the spectrum, I have mentioned those who revel in systematic thinking, but who do not find it easy to apply their thoughts to practical situations. All of these difficulties are aspects of ourselves that we bring to the study of theology. But if we find the study of theology difficult, we should not think that these difficulties lie solely with the theological student. Sometimes the problem is with the theologian we are reading, and students constantly need to discern the merits of whatever 'theology' they are reading.

As I have already said, much that goes by the name of 'theology' is not theology at all. But we also have to contend with a second and opposite problem among systematic theologians. For just as students sometimes want to oversimplify theology by learning set formulas, those whose task it is to systematise our beliefs can also be tempted by the desire to create closed systems that have all the answers.

Just recently I was reading a book by one of our leading contemporary theologians, in which he kept insisting that it is necessary to get our doctrine 'right'. His basic argument was that too many Christians have false ideas about things like the resurrection and ascension of Jesus, and this hinders their ability to apply these doctrines to pastoral and social needs today. Now there is certainly some truth in this assertion: no-one can claim to have mastered such great mysteries at all adequately. But the problem with this particular theologian is that he did not realise that this is true of him as well. He thought that there was a 'right' answer (his, of course!), and that if everyone followed his advice there would be no more difficulties. Yet by trying to pin things down too much, he was in danger not only of getting it wrong, but of losing the plot altogether. By all means let us say what can and must be said, but let us also remember that there are times when healthy agnosticism is preferable to a watertight solution that does not do justice to its subject.

Systematicians who have all the answers are just as useless as systematicians who have none – the trick is to strike the right balance, and it is here that our biblical studies come into play most effectively. Scripture has been given to us as an adequate guide, but not as an exhaustive explanation of every detail. Where it speaks, we must speak; where it is silent, it behoves us to be silent as well. If we can bear that in mind, we shall not go very far wrong nor be led wildly astray. We may not always be absolutely 'right' as our over-confident theologian would like us to be, but we shall be heading in the right direction – towards the worship and praise of Almighty God that he so much wants us to have and enjoy.

Loving God amid theology's 'abstractness'
The final issue we have to discuss is more personal, but it is one that often hits students who choose systematic theology as an option for study. This is the problem of relating our own spiritual experience and relationship with God to a more objective, abstract experience of him.

Some people face similar problems in human life, and it may help to look at them first. For example, a doctor has to treat his patients in an 'objective' manner, facing the realities of their condition as dispassionately as possible and prescribing the best course of treatment accordingly. But what if the patient is a close relative? Can we really expect a doctor to treat his mother or his wife with the same detachment as a patient whom he does not know personally? In many walks of life this difficulty is recognised and people are not allowed to have professional dealings with clients or patients to whom they are closely related, but this is not an option for the systematic theologian. Somehow we have to analyse a God to whom we are intimately connected without losing the relationship or compromising the validity of the analysis. How can we do this?

One way to tackle this question is to look at our own families first. Most of us know that there are things about our closest relations that outsiders are unaware of or may look at differently. For example, my parents may have been first-generation immigrants who escaped poverty elsewhere and struggled for many years to establish themselves in what to them was a foreign land. Social analysts may see them as victims of oppression, discrimination, economic injustice and so on – and they may be right. But I may be only vaguely conscious of these other factors: to me, they remain loving parents who were trying to do their best for their family. The first thing to bear in mind here is that these different points of view are not mutually exclusive. They can both be true in their own way, even if we find it difficult to harmonise them in our own minds. We should not reject the 'objective' analysis merely because it ignores the subjective dimension of our own experience, but neither should we be content to let it be the final word. Our parents are greater than such analyses. They are multi-dimensional people who have to be seen in their fullness if they are to be properly understood and appreciated. Reducing them to only one dimension diminishes them as people and makes it harder to appreciate them for what they are. For we who have known them intimately, finding out these other aspects of their lives ought to increase our admiration and love for them. For those who see only the external analysis, hearing the intimate side is a useful corrective to the tendency to regard them as mere statistics, or cogs in an economic machine. In other words, more points of view should enrich our knowledge, not impoverish or invalidate it.

Now think of God. Those of us who know him intimately cannot and should not try to deny this. We have experienced him as a loving heavenly Father who has saved us from our sins by sending his Son Jesus Christ to die for us and by filling us with his Holy Spirit. That experiential knowledge is vitally important to us and must remain our starting point because it is that which has (probably) led us to want to study theology in the first place. What do we do when we discover that God is a spiritual being with particular attributes like love and justice which may be difficult to harmonise in specific instances? How do we react when we are told that a God of love would not send disease, famine or natural disasters to afflict his creation? What, in other words, do we say when we are confronted with statements about God that seem to go against what we know about him, or when people try to deny his very existence?

If we faced this dilemma with our human parents, we would first ask them for an explanation of the apparent contradiction; and that is what we should do with God. There are always many things about him that we do not know, and before we reject the beliefs we have, we ought at least to go to him in prayer and in the reading of his word and ask him to explain himself to us. This is not a new idea – Anselm of Canterbury (1033–1109) recommended exactly the same technique as the sure guide to all serious theology and called it 'faith seeking understanding'. It has a long and honourable pedigree in Christian thought and we should be grateful for that – and make use of it. Secondly, we should look for inconsistencies in our opponents' arguments. A very useful primer for learning how to do this is C.S. Lewis's book, *Miracles*. Lewis went through all the stock scientific objections to Christianity and demolished them one by one, by showing that they were internally inconsistent. It is only too easy for armchair atheists to take pot-shots at God without considering the limitations of their own perspectives, and we must make ourselves as aware of this as we can.

Thirdly, we should admit that there are some things that we do not understand and never will, but remind ourselves that this is true in a positive as well as in a negative sense. I do not know why there are natural disasters that claim thousands of apparently innocent victims, but neither do I know why God has loved me and saved me in spite of my own unworthiness. The greatest mystery about God is not his justice or his judgment, but his love. For the Almighty ruler of the universe to crush what he has made, either because it is unworthy of him or because he has the power to do with it whatever he wants, is not really very surprising, since we behave in exactly the same way with the things we make or own. But for God to love what is unworthy of him and to rescue it from oblivion – why would he want to do a thing like that? This is the real puzzle, and expressing it turns the critics' arguments on their heads.

In dealing with attacks of this kind, we must remember that we have the same advantage that we have when we confront theories about our migrant parents. We see the issues from another angle, not necessarily denying the supposedly 'objective' accounts but qualifying them by adding a dimension not previously taken into consideration. Of course the critics are free to reject what we have to say and many of them do, but they are the ones who are losing out by failing to take an important piece of evidence into consideration. The Bible does not speak of God in a detached, philosophical manner. It presents us with a challenge: 'Taste and see that the Lord is good' [Ps. 34:8]. Those who have not, cannot or will not do that can never make any authoritative pronouncement on the God of the Bible because they have not engaged with him on the Bible's own terms. The world is full of scholars who know all about love, marriage and family from a theoretical point of view – but who then discover that their perspectives change radically when they embark on that path for themselves. ('The problem with books about having babies,' a friend once told me, 'is that the babies haven't read the books.') In the end, nothing beats experience, and here the believer is streets ahead of his opponents. For me to say that God does not exist because I have never met him is as absurd as saying that you do not exist because I have never met you. But the only way I can ever know you is by accepting you on your own terms – if I insist that you must be James Bond or Cinderella in order to be 'real', I am never going to find you however hard I look. This is what atheists and agnostics do with God, and a little thought will show just how foolish their approach is.

Of course, knowing the real you is not without its problems, since real people are always much more complex than fictitious characters are. Living in a fantasy world, as many people do, is often easier and more enjoyable than the real thing because we are not challenged to think twice about our assumptions – James Bond and Cinderella are so much more predictable, and therefore more controllable, than the people I have to live with every day. Real knowledge of real people is all about being challenged, as any married couple or parent can tell you. The real God is much more exciting than any philosophical caricature precisely because he is so challenging: he wants us to go back to square one with our assumptions – to be 'born again', as Jesus puts it [John 3:3]. And the great thing is that if you are a believer, then that has already happened to you before you begin the serious business of analysing the creator of the reality in which we live.

Conclusion

The challenge of theology will never go away because challenge is the trigger to growth, and as Christians we are called to grow in our knowledge and understanding of God. But if we tackle this in the right way, with the right assumptions, we shall not be disappointed or puzzled for long. The Lord rewards those who diligently seek him [Matt. 7:7-11]. It is up to us to start looking.

11

The Trials of Christian Ethics

Dennis P. Hollinger

A theological student has begun to 'digest' the early stages of theological study. The steeper parts of the theological learning curve have begun to flatten out, and armed with some knowledge of the Scriptures and with some basic building blocks of theological thought, we turn our attention to ethics. But we are shocked at what we find. We feel as if we are back at 'square one', with almost no capacity to integrate the incredible complexities of this subject. We find it almost impossible to bring our theological thinking to bear on all that. We feel pressured to change, yet are simultaneously stuck in the bog of endless moral possibilities.

Dr Dennis P. Hollinger, President and Coleman M. Mockler Distinguished Professor of Christian Ethics at Gordon-Conwell Theological Seminary in South Hamilton, Massachusetts, shows how the complexity of ethics is not necessarily a surrender to moral relativism. He outlines the modes of ethical thought that we bring to this subject, and contrasts the way that the knowledge of the Triune God and of the Christian worldview gives different moral outcomes.

Theological ethics is at its best only an extension of a kind of Scripturally-based theological thinking. It is hard, but it is doable, and the pastor who does it can become adept at showing others how the gospel decodes the everyday assumptions and practices that surround us, giving us surprising new options for navigating our lives.

Disorientated by ethics

War. Homosexuality. Torture of prisoners. Racial and ethnic justice. Cloning. Poverty. Artificial insemination. Business ethics. Premarital sex. These are just a few of the many
ethical issues facing contemporary church, society and individuals. Theological students beginning to face these and
other issues head-on can feel quite threatened by various
challenges.

First, the serious study of ethics challenges the settled
positions we bring to it. When positions that once seemed
clearly 'black' or 'white' are interrogated, we are left reeling.
When we look at the varying ways that the world and even
portions of the Church respond to ethical issues, one is
tempted to believe that there is no right and wrong. Many
assume that complex issues mandate an ethical relativism,
the belief that 'what is right and wrong, good and bad,
true and false varies from time to time, place to place, and
person to person. There are no absolute standards of truth or
morality.'[1] Students can easily feel as if they are being steered
towards or are becoming mired in this kind of relativism.

To be sure there is often a complexity to issues, meaning
that there may be competing ethical principles or virtues,
varying interpretations of the facts surrounding an issue,
or differing strategies in how to address the issue. But
complexity and ethical relativism are two different things.

Ethical relativism in the modern and now postmodern
world has been fuelled by the growing pluralism of our
cultures. Today we daily rub shoulders with people who
have diverse worldviews and moral frameworks. In such

1. E. David Cook, 'Relativism', in *New Dictionary of Christian Ethics and Pastoral
   Theology*, ed. David J. Atkinson (Downers Grove, IL: Inter Varsity Press,
   1995), p. 726.

cultures there is frequently a growing secularisation in which religious norms and standards are relegated to the periphery of society or the private spheres of life. Religious forces play a significant role in personal dimensions of existence, but are deemed inappropriate for the public square of politics, business, education, law and medicine. Many therefore assume that there can be no common approach to finding the good and right in the midst of the perplexing issues of our time. This milieu can lead to a second kind of concern for students – in this case, a form of melancholy. 'What is the point,' we might ask ourselves, 'of trying to insert a Christian ethic into this social mix?' Christians become defensive, fearful, resigned or despairing about the marginalisation of a Christian account of ethics – rather than seeing the Christian worldview and its ethic as the unanticipated good news that every society needs.

Christian faith (and many other systems of ethics as well) assumes that there are divine givens to which our lives ought to conform. There are realities external to ourselves towards which our behaviour, character and thinking are to be directed. When students start to see these realities, a third problem can emerge: we feel unpleasantly constrained, so that ethics becomes a burdensome task or set of duties under some 'rule of law'. That kind of conclusion is not the way the Scriptures talk of ethics. The biblical authors think that our proper description of and participation in these external realities releases us into the best kind of freedom.

But this unpleasant sense of constraint is in all likelihood driven by another major shift underlying contemporary pluralistic relativism. In our postmodern world divine or even natural givens are often rejected and replaced by a more subjective approach to ethics and morality. Now we seek to conform the external world to our own subjective feelings and desires. Rather than seeking to orient our behaviour to a norm beyond ourselves, we seek to orient the norms to our own self-referential existence.

This shift was particularly made possible by the modern world's desire and capacity to reshape the external world by the ingenuity and power of mind and will (a habit of thought sometimes called 'voluntarism'). Modern scientific understandings and technological achievements allow humans a much greater ability to shape the external world towards a desired end or goal. Thus, we have the capacity to reshape offspring through new reproductive technologies. We have the capacity to even restructure gender through biomedical procedures. This means that the world today increasingly seeks to shape human identity according to human desires. Dale Kuehne coins the term 'iWorld' to describe our individualistic postmodern world. 'In the iWorld,' he says, 'identity is something we are instructed to select or create. If we don't like or aren't comfortable with who we are, we are encouraged to remake ourselves in whatever manner we are able and science will allow.'[2] For students embedded in the voluntarist 'iWorld', Christian ethics can seem like a threat to our self-chosen identity. (In a way, it *is* a threat while we are being inducted into and are taking on our new identity – that of Jesus Christ.)

Given these difficulties inherent to the study of ethics, I thought it might be helpful to offer a summary outline of the way ethics presents itself to us in our culture. I will then summarise the way ethics arises from the Christian gospel.

---

2.   Dale S. Kuehne, *Sex and the iWorld: Rethinking Relationship Beyond an Age of Individualism* (Grand Rapids: Baker, 2009), p. 139.

These approaches to life both offer and account for different answers to questions such as 'what is right and good? What is it that makes our actions and character virtuous and just? And how do we know the right, good, virtuous and just?'

'Families' of ethical theory

There have been many ethical theories developed over the years, but essentially they fall into three categories or families for determining ethical norms and actions. Each of these families of ethics has differing conceptions of the foundation for ethics, how we know or establish moral norms, and how we make ethical decisions. The three main families or categories are consequential ethics, principle ethics and character or virtue ethics.

Consequential Ethics

Many people assume that ethics can only be established by the results of their actions. Here there is no intrinsic right or wrong and there are no inherent norms or ethical duties to guide. Ethics is essentially the attempt to calculate the results that flow from our choices. Most thinkers in this camp contend that all humans naturally seek for happiness and pleasure in life, and thus the consequences are calculated in terms of happiness, pleasure or human interests. But this of course begs the question: happiness or pleasure for whom? Essentially there are two responses.

Some contend that the calculation of consequences is with reference to the individual making the choice. This is frequently called *ethical egoism*. Many individuals in our world pursue life with a perspective, 'What's in it for me?' 'What will bring me the greatest happiness?' But this is not just a popular, unthinking way to do ethics. It has a long history going back to the philosopher Epicurus (341–270 B.C.) who espoused hedonism, the notion that pleasure for oneself is the highest good. It was brilliantly argued by Ayn Rand, the Russian-born novelist and philosopher in the twentieth century, with her defence of 'rational self-interest'. The ethical egoist argues that as long as no one gets hurt, each pursuing their own interest will actually be best for society as a whole.

The other form of consequentialism is *utilitarianism*. Here the focus is not on pleasure or happiness for me, but rather for all who are impacted by my decision. The mantra of utilitarianism is, 'The greatest good for the greatest number of people.' Jeremy Bentham in the nineteenth century actually developed a calculus for determining the greatest amount of good (defined as happiness or pleasure) for the greatest number. Ethics had essentially become mathematics.

Today one of the best-known utilitarians is the Australian philosopher Peter Singer, now teaching moral philosophy at Princeton University. Singer suggests the language of interest in place of happiness or pleasure and says, 'In place of my own interests, I now have to take into account the interests of all those affected by my decision. This requires me to weigh up all these interests and adopt the course of action most likely to maximise the interests of those affected.'[3] It is through this procedure that Singer has become infamous for his strident defence of animal rights, his support for the euthanasia of some deformed children, and his openness to sex with animals.

We, of course, hope that our ethical choices in life will lead to positive results for us and for others. But consequen-

---

3.   Peter Singer, *Writings on an Ethical Life* (New York: Ecco, 2000), p. 16.

tialism as an ethical foundation and methodology is highly problematic. For one thing it easily leads to an ends-justi-fies-the-means ethic, and some of the world's worst atrocities have been legitimised on such grounds. Furthermore, it overlooks the reality that some things in life are intrinsically good and ought to be pursued regardless of the outcome. We pursue love, justice, purity and integrity not because they produce good results, but because they are worthy pursuits through which we honour God. Some would even argue that if God were not in the picture we intuitively know that these are intrinsically good. Consequentialism rejects this basic view of life.

Principle Ethics
A second foundation for ethics is principle ethics, sometimes called deontological ethics, coming from a Greek word for duty. In this approach there are actions that are inherently good or bad, just and unjust. We have a duty in life to perform good and virtuous actions, and we know these through basic moral principles or rules. These principles can be derived from several different sources: reason, tradition, universal human experience or divine revelation. While there are universal principles to guide us in life, many principle ethicists would contend that at times principles can be in conflict. (A good example comes from World War II when some people hid Jews in their homes, and when questioned by the Gestapo, were faced with a conflict of principles: telling the truth versus the preservation of human life.)

Numerous philosophers have defended a deontological ethic on the basis of reason, including Socrates and Kant. Living in the eighteenth century, Kant grew up in a pietistic Christian home, but rejected the faith in favour of

Enlightenment rationalism when he went off to university. He came to believe that God was not needed for discerning ethical guidelines, for reason alone could lead to fundamental principles from which other principles could be derived. On this basis Kant strongly defended fairly traditional ethical norms such as honesty and fidelity in marriage.

Some Christian traditions have also articulated a principle ethic with a significant use of human reason. This is particularly evident in the Roman Catholic tradition with an emphasis on natural law, said to be evident to all humans apart from saving grace or special revelation in Christ and the Bible. Because all humans can know God's law through nature there can be an expectation of fairly significant obedience to God's natural law in all societies, including in their civil laws.

Other Christian theologians and ethicists have articulated a principle approach to ethics using primarily Scripture. They contend that the Ten Commandments, prophetic injunctions, the Proverbs, the Sermon on the Mount and Pauline principles all call believers to follow very clear and concrete rules of behaviour in life. John Calvin, the sixteenth century Reformer believed that the moral law of God was rooted in the character of God, but the law was the heart of ethical decision-making. 'Everything relating to a perfect rule of life the Lord has so comprehended in his law, that he has left nothing for men to add to the summary there given.'[4] He argued that while the law *per se* doesn't explicitly give us every ethical principle, from it we can derive other principles that pertain to every sphere of life in this world.

There is no question that God's written word gives us ethical principles and guidance for our lives. But many rightly

---

4.   Calvin, *Institutes* IV.x.7.

ask the question, 'Are these principles the foundation for our ethics?' They certainly show us the path we should follow in various spheres of living, but are they really the heart of Christian ethics? After all the Pharisees followed the law of God meticulously but Jesus strongly questioned their ethics, noting, 'These people honour me with their lips, but their hearts are far from me' [Matt. 15:8].

The main problem historically with principle ethics is the failure to set the principles in a larger context or narrative. Principles show us the way we ought to live, but not why we ought to live that way. They do not get to the heart of what makes our actions good, right, just and virtuous. We do well to remember that the Ten Commandments begin with a prologue which forms the larger narrative and grounding for the commands themselves: 'I am the Lord your God, who brought you out of Egypt, out of the land of slavery' [Exod. 20:2]. If we make principles and laws the foundation rather than the vehicles of ethical guidance, we easily end up with legalism – law for law's sake. We miss the primary nature of the good and the proper motivation for doing the good.

Character/Virtue Ethics

In recent decades a number of theologians and ethicists have espoused a new approach to ethics, or better a renewal of an old approach. Going back to the ethics of Aristotle these folks contend that utilitarian and principle approaches to ethics ask the wrong question. The issue is not, 'What should I do?' but rather, 'Who should I be?' These thinkers contend that the heart of ethics is not about our actions but our character and the inner virtues that constitute our character.

Character ethics stresses that our actions automatically flow from our character. Character is essentially forged in a given community through narratives that form the heart and identity of that community. The communal narratives then implicitly teach virtues and vices that become internalised in the lives of the community's members. It follows that as Iris Murdoch once put it, 'At crucial moments of choice, most of the business of choosing is already over.'[5]

The best-known Christian virtue ethicist today is Stanley Hauerwas of Duke University Divinity School in Durham, North Carolina. Hauerwas contends that there is no such thing as ethics per se, for there must always be a qualifier reflecting a community and its narratives. Thus we can speak of Christian ethics, Buddhist ethics, humanistic ethics, Enlightenment ethics, etc., but not a universal ethic. Hauerwas has a strong aversion to principle ethics and especially those grounded in human reason. For Hauerwas the key issue is not what we do when faced with ethical decisions, but who we are as we face them. Christian ethical behaviour flows from our inner character, shaped by the Jesus story embedded in the life of the Church.

Character or virtue ethics has much to commend to Christians. Advocates are right to remind us that there is always a larger narrative or framework to our ethic or even to the principles in our ethic. Moreover, their emphasis on character is an important element of ethical living, for the entire Bible emphasises the role of the heart and our inner selves in our actions [Matt. 15:17-20]. The community context is also vital for the development of character and moral action. We best forge a Christian character in the context of the Church.

There are, however, some weaknesses to the way character ethics is frequently formulated. While character is essential

---

5. Iris Murdoch, *The Sovereignty of Good* (New York: Schocken Books, 1971), p. 37.

for ethics, why does it need to be set over against behavioural forms of ethics? It may be better to formulate an ethic in which actions and character go together, both influencing the other. Also, we need to question whether narrative alone is sufficient. The Scriptures come to us in a broad array of genre: narrative, prophetic injunctions, proverbs, epistolary exhortations, poetry, history, and apocalyptic imagery. All of these are part of God's divine revelation and all provide norms for Christian ethics.

Another framework: God and the Christian worldview
Though there is much we learn from the traditional theories of ethics, we need, I believe, another approach for Christian ethics. From biblical and theological perspectives there is an ultimate foundation and then a secondary foundation for determining the right, good and just. The ultimate foundation is the triune God and the secondary foundation is the Christian worldview derived from God's Word, incarnate and written.

The Triune God
The triune God is the ultimate foundation of all reality, including ethics. Moral goodness and justice flow from the very character and actions of God. Why is love a virtue and an essential principle for life and relationships? Ultimately because God is love [1 John 4:10-11]. Why are we to act justly towards the poor and disenfranchised? Because God did just that for his people [Deut. 15:15]. Why are we to live lives of holiness? Because God is holy [Lev. 20:26]. Why are we to live in covenant faithfulness to our spouses? Because God is a covenant God, faithful to his people, even when they were unfaithful [Hosea 1–3; Mal. 2:10, 14].

Ultimately, goodness, rightness and justice are not established by principles but rather by the God behind those principles. We are called to lives of mercy, justice, integrity, holiness and purity, not because of any consequences that might flow from them or because our own communities espouse them. Rather, the very virtues and norms themselves flow from our Creator, Redeemer and Sustainer. Thus, ultimately we do the right things in life because we reflect and honour God in doing so. And what God has designed in accordance with his character and actions are the very best paths to daily living.

The Christian Worldview
But there is a second foundation that is very important in providing norms and direction to our moral lives and ethical choices as Christians – the Christian worldview. All ethics flows out of our worldview – that is, our set of basic assumptions about ultimate reality, human nature, the fundamental problem of humanity, the solution to that problem, and our view of where history is headed. All of these assumptions deeply impact what we believe is right, good and just, and profoundly direct our daily choices and actions.

For the Christian the essential worldview, or biblical narrative, can be set forth with four main components: creation, fall, redemption and consummation. In a sense every worldview embodies these elements, and the substance of these conceptions influences one's ethic.

A theology of creation is not only essential for Christian theology, but also for Christian ethics. At the heart of the biblical narrative is the story of a good God who creates a good world, with human beings at the apex of this creation. Several dimensions of creation give substance and direction to ethical issues. One is God's pronouncement of his creation as good [Gen. 1:21]. The physical world, the human body, and the essential institutions of culture and society are good gifts of God; not major deterrents to Christian faithfulness. The fall, of course, wreaks havoc with all of reality, but the goodness of creation reminds us that God has called us to live in his world, not to abandon it.

A second element of creation is man and woman created in the image of God. The *imago dei* has long been an issue of exegetical and theological debate, but there are several interpretations that are salient for ethics. For one, it implies that humans are set apart from the rest of the created order and hence have an intrinsic dignity and value that is to be protected in every sphere of life. The *imago dei* also implies a creation care foundation, for just as God in his providence cares for all creation, so we are given a cultural mandate to represent him in our care of creation. There is also a relational dimension to the image of God, for just as God exists in an eternal relationship of love between Father, Son and Holy Spirit, so we are created for relationship as males and females [Gen. 1:27]. Thus, the doctrine of the image of God carries norms and guidance for a broad array of ethical issues: race relations, sexual ethics, bioethics and environmental ethics.

Though creation is a vital element of the Christian worldview, it is evident that things are 'not the way (they're) supposed to be'.[6] The fall into human sin and brokenness is the second main part of the Christian worldview. As is evident from the story of the fall in Genesis 3, every dimension of the world and every aspect of human life have been impacted by sin. Though God's 'good' creation still exists we distort his good gifts, using them in ways our Maker never intended.

---

6. The phrase is taken from Cornelius Plantinga Jr, *Not the Way It's Supposed to Be: A Breviary of Sin* (Grand Rapids: Eerdmans, 1995).

Though the image of God still resides in all human beings we now destroy his good creation, exploit our fellow creatures and use our creativity for idolatrous purposes.

The fall has not destroyed God's creation work, but 'sin and evil always have the character of caricature ... a distorted image that nevertheless embodies certain recognizable features.' Thus:

> A human being after the fall, though a travesty of humanity, is still a human being, not an animal. A humanistic school is still a school. A broken relationship is still a relationship. Muddled thinking is still thinking. In each case, what something in a fallen creation 'still is' points to the enduring goodness of creation.[7]

This understanding of the fall means that Christians are not called away from the fallen world, but to faithfulness to God and his moral designs while living in the midst of the world.

The fall also reminds us that we can never be utopian in our perceptions of the world and in our efforts to change the way things are. Just as self-deception occurs in the story of the fall [Gen. 3:12-13], so utopian attempts to achieve justice and goodness in the world have ended up with incredible injustices and evil precisely because of self-deception. The account we give of human nature has a powerful impact upon ethical thought and action, including our political ethics. Too high an account of the human and cultural possibilities leads us to impossible dreams that can come back to haunt us. Conversely, a bestial view of human nature and overly negative view of society can lead us to despair and a loss of dignity in human relations. An ethic grounded in a Christian

---

7. Albert Wolters, *Creation Regained*, 2nd edition (Grand Rapids: Eerdmans, 2005), p. 58.

worldview must always hold together two dimensions of human nature: wonderfully made and terribly fallen.

The third part of the biblical drama and the Christian worldview is redemption. In the biblical story, after the fall God begins a process of redemption that culminates in the coming of the Messiah. It is through the death and resurrection of Christ that God makes possible a forgiveness of human sin and an empowerment and new perspective for ethical character and action. While most every worldview gives some kind of solution to the human malaise, in the biblical account the solution is redemption in Christ.

In redemption the very righteousness of Christ is imputed to the believer and counts as our righteousness before God. But salvation embodies more than a forensic justification of right standing before the Creator. Christ's work in an individual's life is transformative through the work of the Holy Spirit. There is an ongoing work of redemption, sanctification, in which individuals' hearts, minds and actions are made new through Christ. No moral solution in this world is as powerful as redemption in Christ with the Spirit's empowerment. Thus, Christians should be more just, loving, merciful, and faithful because of the transcendent work of God within.

This salvation is not, however, individualistic. Sanctification itself is to spill over into social realities. As John Wesley put it, 'Solitary religion is not found (in the gospel). "Holy solitaries" is a phrase no more consistent with the gospel than "holy adulterers". The gospel of Christ knows no religion but social; no holiness but social holiness.'[8] God's

---

8. Quoted in Leon Hynson, *To Reform the Nation: Theological Foundations of Wesley's Ethics* (Grand Rapids: Zondervan, 1984), p. 9.

redemptive work in the world even has cosmic ramifications, for 'the creation itself will be liberated from its bondage to decay and brought into the glorious freedom of the children of God' [Rom. 8:21]. Redemption has social implications, for God is at work through his people now to be salt and light in a world that has lost its way ethically. At times God uses his common grace meted out to all humanity to control sin and injustice in the world, but the salvific grace through Christ is God's ultimate solution to the fallen world.

The final part of the biblical drama and a Christian worldview is the consummation. It is evident that God's work of redemption has been fully accomplished through Christ's work on the cross, but the full effect of that redemption awaits the *eschaton*. Our perceptions of the *eschaton* or where history is headed has a powerful impact upon ethics.

Some Christians have had a very optimistic view of history, in which humans bring God's kingdom to earth by transforming the institutions of society. This has sometimes resulted in a triumphalism that equates human efforts and ideologies with God's work. Others have had an extremely negative and pessimistic view of history in which believers can do nothing about societal evils, except to bring individuals to Christ and await his coming. Between these two extremes is an understanding that the fullness of the kingdom awaits the final consummation. But we are called now to live our lives in light of that coming kingdom, and bear witness to God's final transformation.

A future kingdom is not cause for passivity, for as John put it, 'All who have this hope in him purify themselves' [1 John 3:3 NRSV]. The future hope guides ethical behaviour now, including an entrance into the broken world as salt and light. But the

Christian's efforts to change the world are always in light of the final transformation. The future hope relativises the world and all present efforts to change it. 'Absolute justice (or equality, peace, etc.) will occur at the return of Christ and only then. This frees us in the present from idolatries, perfectionism, utopian schemes and absolutizing of positions, parties, nations and ideologies. Perfection comes only at the end.'[9]

Conclusion

We face great ethical and moral challenges in contemporary society. In the midst of these challenges Christians need a firm foundation and framework to guide and sustain them. The traditional paradigms of consequential ethics and principle ethics offer some wisdom, but in the end are not satisfactory. Character ethics with its emphasis on virtues cultivated by narratives in a community context are part of the equation, but not the whole.

Ultimately we must recognise that our foundation is the triune God. The actions and character of God form the heart and basis for our ethical stance and motivation. Coupled with the ultimate foundation is the Christian worldview that provides rich wisdom and guidance for the journey. Creation, fall, redemption and consummation are not abstract theological tenets. They form a secondary foundation and rich direction for the many ethical issues we find in our world.

Some difficulties do emerge in the serious study of ethics. Mentally, it is complex. Socially, a Christian view can seem marginalised. Personally, changes to our identity and practices are very confronting.

---

9. David W. Gill, 'Hope', in *New Dictionary of Christian Ethics and Pastoral Theology*, ed. David Atkinson (Downers Grove, IL: InterVarsity Press, 1995), p. 456.

Yet it is worth persevering. We wrestle with how the triune God and the Christian worldview give us new ways to see and navigate moral complexity. The character of God and the Christian worldview both enable us to integrate and interpret clamouring moral voices. We also discover that changes to our 'identity' are not as threatening as they might at first seem. We begin to see that truly we are being freed into a better way of life. We learn new ways to describe moral problems, new 'tools' to untangle them, and new suggestions for better ways forward.

The Christian gospel brings unanticipated and badly needed news to a struggling world. The study of theological ethics shows how the gospel applies in the cut-and-thrust of everyday life.

Lost For Words

The study of theology is arguably the most demanding discipline in the academy. Faculties of theology have been around in European universities from their very foundation. The University of Aberdeen in Scotland, for example, where I taught in the 1990s, celebrated its Quincentenary in 1995. Only two disciplines lasted the full five hundred years: medicine and divinity.

Theology is the interdisciplinary subject par excellence. With good reason earlier generations called it 'the Queen of the Sciences'. To study theology you need an unrivalled range of knowledge and skills: archaeology, linguistics, anthropology, an acquaintance with every period of history, not to mention classics, Judaica, cultural studies, hermeneutics, and so forth.

Theology also has the most intensely practical and personal as well as the most sweeping and lofty questions to answer. The upside is that students experience genuine intellectual satisfaction when finally they nail a theme or topic, write that erudite essay, give that scintillating seminar paper, or preach that enlightening sermon. The apostle Paul could certainly have felt the glow when he wrote what Samuel Taylor Coleridge called the most profound book in existence, the letter to the Romans.

If Romans is a masterpiece, to mix my metaphors, chapters 9–11 are the jewel in the crown. Here Paul treats the most burning question for Christians in the first century, namely, the place of Israel in God's plan of salvation. His answer is the high point of his theology.

Far from an excursus or aside in the letter, Romans 9–11 is the key section. It addresses head-on some major concerns arising from his earlier argument. If in Romans 1:16 the gospel is to the Jew first, *why* has there been so little response among Jews? If in Romans 3:1–2 the Jews enjoy so many privileges, *what has happened* to the divine promises? The apostle finds that some presume to put God in the dock, accusing him of unrighteousness.

He bravely takes on the role of legal advocate, and in the Bible's ultimate theodicy, he establishes God's innocence. Paul's intricate argument makes the case that despite Israel's rejection of the righteousness of God that is by faith, and despite her temporary rejection by God, God still remains faithful to his covenant promises. In God's defence Paul quotes the Old Testament more than thirty times, pointing to God's 'mercy' as the answer to the conundrum of Israel's hardening. The word 'mercy', which in the rest of Paul's letters combined makes only eight appearances, occurs no fewer than seven times in these three chapters. So, far from being an interruption or a distracting detour the three chapters deal with matters most profound, such as election and reprobation, and divine sovereignty and human responsibility. Speaking humanly, Paul is to be congratulated for writing them.

As Luther puts it, doctrines such as those in Romans 9–11 are not milk but are solid food for the mature. This means that even those who seriously and properly wrestle with this material get to bask in reflected glory. For example, according to Charles Cranfield (the Emeritus Professor in Theology at Durham University), Karl Barth's *Church Dogmatics* exposition of this section of Romans 'would have been enough by itself to place its author among the greatest theologians of the Church, even if he had written nothing else.'[1]

To do justice in this way to such sections of Scripture is surely the goal of every serious student of theology. But amazingly, *all* we are doing in such moments, even at our best and finest, is seeking to plumb 'the depth of the riches of the wisdom and knowledge of God' [Rom 11:33a]. For despite its genius, Romans 9–11 itself only ends with a shake of the head, in praise and wonder of God.

Of all of Paul's doxologies, only Romans 11:33–36 begins with a surprised interjection, 'Oh!' It then continues with three rapturous exclamations and three humbling rhetorical questions:

> Oh, the depth of the riches of the wisdom and knowledge of God!
> How unsearchable his judgments,
> and his paths beyond tracing out!
> Who has known the mind of the Lord?
> Or who has been his counsellor?
> Who has ever given to God, that God should repay him?
> For from him and through him and to him are all things.
> To him be the glory forever! Amen.

Now at this point we might even wonder – why the 'Oh!'? And what could possibly remain 'unsearchable', 'unfathomable' and 'untraceable'? Surely Paul's intricate argument already 'got to the bottom' of what needed to be known. But

---

1. Charles E.B. Cranfield, *A Critical and Exegetical Commentary on the Epistle to the Romans, Volume 2* (Edinburgh: T. & T. Clark, 1979), p. 449.

in these eloquent verses, Paul finds himself moved to praise God's ultimately mysterious judgments and ways. Having composed the most profound, orthodox and faultless reflection on the most enigmatic actions of God, Paul is frankly forced to admit that his thoughts do not conform to those of God.

Here we learn that theology, in contrast to many other disciplines, never completely comprehends its subject. God is not like the biologist's 'specimen' or the historian's 'era' or the archaeologist's 'dig'. In each of these, even when some unknowns are left, one can still 'arrive' at a point where the object of study can truly be said to be 'known'. But God's activity cannot be judged from any such higher vantage point, and in the final analysis, he cannot be figured out. This is because, as verses 34–35 put it, no one knows the mind of the Lord or is able to give him advice.

We must not miss the irony of Paul's admission here. It follows one of Christianity's best minds having just written his most inspired exposition. The reality is that God's transcendence demands that we admit that our discourse about God is at best approximate. Our interpretation may be accurate, but if we grasped the full perspective it would literally blow our minds.

Paul's spontaneous eruptions of praise in Romans 11:33-36 point to a potent danger for students of theology, that is, of substituting intellectual stimulation for genuine spiritual experience. Studying theology without arriving at wonder is like growing a rose bush and producing only thorns and prickles. It is all voyage and no destination. It is like travelling to Arizona, pondering the geology of the Grand Canyon, memorizing its dimensions, editing the tourist video, but forgetting to take a look. It is like struggling all the way to

Bakken – then having no idea how to enjoy it (pp. 10–11 above).

When Paul turns to prayer on two other occasions in his letters, without undermining the truth of his theological discussions, he underscores two things: the fact that God and his work exceed human comprehension; and the goal of thanks and praise. 'First I pray that you … [might] grasp how wide and long and high and deep is the love of Christ, and to know this love that *surpasses knowledge* … [T]o him be the glory' [Eph. 3:17-19, 21]. Even if 'knowing' Christ's love in all its vastness is his petition, paradoxically Paul confesses that Christ's love 'surpasses knowledge'. And second: 'Thanks be to God for his *indescribable* gift' [2 Cor. 9:15]. Even if the magnificent gift of salvation and wisdom for living that is embodied in Christ is the object of study for true theology, ultimately this gift is 'indescribable'. Theologians must never forget that the task of theology is to know the unknowable and to describe the indescribable.

As these passages demonstrate, the hard work of thinking about God in the light of his revelation, rightly undertaken, does not replace but rather provokes the sublime experience of praise and wonder in the presence of God. Students do well to remember that the goal of our theological study is not to figure out God, but rather, to arrive at awestruck incredulity and joyful confidence in God. It is to be blown away in wide-eyed, transfixed adoration. To miss that is to miss everything and to fail to glorify God in our studies. The aim is not finally an accurate eloquence, but to become *lost for words*, in the praise and wonder of God.

Brian S. Rosner (with Andrew Cameron)
Moore Theological College
Sydney, October 2009

Christian Focus Publications

publishes books for all ages

Our mission statement –

STAYING FAITHFUL

In dependence upon God we seek to impact the world through literature faithful to His infallible Word, the Bible. Our aim is to ensure that the LORD Jesus Christ is presented as the only hope to obtain forgiveness of sin, live a useful life and look forward to heaven with Him.

REACHING OUT

Christ's last command requires us to reach out to our world with His gospel. We seek to help fulfil that by publishing books that point people towards Jesus and help them develop a Christ-like maturity. We aim to equip all levels of readers for life, work, ministry and mission.

Books in our adult range are published in three imprints.

Christian Focus contains popular works including biographies, commentaries, basic doctrine and Christian living. Our children's books are also published in this imprint.

Mentor focuses on books written at a level suitable for Bible College and seminary students, pastors, and other serious readers. The imprint includes commentaries, doctrinal studies, examination of current issues and church history.

Christian Heritage contains classic writings from the past.

Christian Focus Publications Ltd,
Geanies House, Fearn, Ross-shire,
IV20 1TW, Scotland, United Kingdom
info@christianfocus.com
www.christianfocus.com